A Life in Two Worlds

Betty Powell Skoog

with

Justine Kerfoot

Paper Moon Publishing

Paper Moon Publishing
Paper Moon, Inc.
7230 S. County Rd. P
Lake Nebagamon, WI
(715) 374-3482

A Life In Two Worlds

Editing, Layout: Judith James
Cover Design: Lisa Wagner
All photos provided by Betty Powell Skoog

Printed in the United States of America by IntraNet Solutions, Inc.

10 9 8 7 6 5 4 3 2

ISBN 0-9653027-1-7
Library of Congress Catalog Card Number: 96-70457

12/18/96 B
Skoog
Sko

Printed on Recycled Paper

Special Thanks
from
Betty Powell - Skoog
to

Shirley Peruniak, Historian
Quetico Provincial Park
Ministry of Natural Resources
Atikokan, Ontario, Canada

- and to -

Justine Kerfoot
for her friendship and help — in my life and with this book.

This book is dedicated to
Tempest Powell Benson
who passed away on January 8, 1996

One cannot think of Tempest without also vividly recalling the wilderness area of Saganaga and the island she made home. Though she was unable to live there the last few years of her life, it is there that God formed her heart and soul, and where, for many of us, our beloved memories of her will remain forevermore. Tempest will forever be in all of our hearts.

A Foreword From The Authors

From my grandparent's home on Saganagons, a journey to the nearest town was a mile by canoe and then a two-and-a-half mile portage to Saganaga Lake. Saganaga Lake was sixteen miles and eight portages from the Gunflint Trail, which in turn extended fifty miles to Grand Marais, the small fishing village on Lake Superior.

My mom, Tempest Powell, had to go to Gunflint Lodge, located at the end of the Gunflint Trail, to get anything she ordered from a catalog. There was no mail service to Gunflint in the mid-1920's. Everyone was dependent on an incoming person asking for the mail at the post office in Grand Marais and then bringing it up to Gunflint when they came.

It was at the Gunflint Lodge where my mom met Justine Spunner Kerfoot, the co-author of this book. Justine and Tempest became lifelong friends.

Betty Powell - Skoog

Betty In Her Tickanoggin At The Age Of Two

*   *   *   *   *

In 1927 when Mother and I crested the last rocky ridge in my Whippet car, the vista to the north opened up, revealing Gunflint Lake on the Minnesota - Canadian border. A vast and untamed wilderness reached in all directions. It seemed like an open door to an unknown adventure that was intriguing, forbidding and challenging.

I was a college student joining my mother as she sought to buy a small resort with a store and 3 log cabins, deep in the woods of northern Minnesota. We traveled on an original, Indian trail extending from Grand Marais and eventually to Gunflint Lake. It had been gradually widened enough to allow for cars and chartered busses when adventurous sportsmen from Chicago had started to find out about this unspoiled fishing and hunting area.

Little did I know that Gunflint was to become my home. In time, I would learn from the Indians how to survive in the wilderness and to know their ways. Eventually, I would earn their trust and they would share some of their lifestyle, knowledge and beliefs with me. One such relationship developed with Tempest Powell and her family.

Justine Kerfoot

In The Beginning

An Introduction by Justine Kerfoot

Where the northeastern section of Minnesota joins with Ontario, Canada, the international boundary follows a waterway interlaced with rivers and lakes. It crosses the Laurentian Divide, which separates the flow of water from Lake Superior and the Hudson Bay watersheds. This Indian highway was traversed by French voyageurs, fur traders, explorers, surveyors, prospectors, loggers and an occasional Catholic Priest. A large portion of this lake country is now designated the Boundary Waters Canoe Area Wilderness in the United States and the Quetico Provincial Park in Canada.

This land was occupied largely by the Ojibwa Indians until 1900. They were surrounded by the Dakotas to the west of the Mississippi River, and to the northwest by the Souix and Assiniboins. The Crees lived to the north along the shores of Hudson Bay, and the Algonquins to the northeast. The Cree fought with the Ojibwa and stole many of their girls and women. As a result, some of our oldest Ojibwa Indians were partly Cree.

Many Indians settled in different areas along the international border, with varying exposures to white people. Twenty-five or thirty Indians lived in the eastern half of the village of Grand Marais. The women made birch bark baskets, often decorated with porcupine quills, buckskin moccasins decorated with beaded flowers, and buckskin vests. The men trapped in winter and guided in summer. Some intermarried with the incoming white people.

A number of the Indians gradually dispersed to Grand Portage: the old staging grounds where furs were brought from the interior and transferred to Lake Superior canoes headed for Fort William (now called Thunder Bay) and the fur market.

The western half of this fishing village was occupied by people of Norwegian and Swedish descent. The men were primarily fishermen and loggers. Their wives brought with them the ethnic recipes now so common to the region — lutefisk, pickled herring, sylta (made from the heads of pigs) and lefsa. A number of these women were teachers in single room schools.

Forty or more Indian families were scattered from Gunflint, Saganaga and Saganagons to Kawnipi Lake and then northeast to Kawa Bay at the mouth of the Ka-Wa-Wi-aga-muk (high bush cranberry) River, where an officially numbered Indian reservation had been established. The chief of the band, Black Stone (Muk-a-day-wa-sin), lived in a log cabin on the reservation. He argued eloquently and repeatedly for the rights of his people both before and after the Treaty of 1873, the third treaty with the Canadian government. Black Stone also found the first producing gold mine in the province of Ontario, called the Moss Mine.

During the winter of 1918 and 1919, many Indians died from influenza, not only at Kawa Bay, but throughout all the Indian camps. The dead were buried in the snow. Black Stone and his woman went for help when so many became ill at Kawa Bay.

They snowshoed across country to Jack Powell's home on Saganagons Lake, hoping to get out the word of their plight, only to find out the radio batteries had run down and there was no outside communication available. They then snowshoed to Joe Russell's store in Ely. Joe wired the Canadian officials that "The Indian village at Kawa Bay is dying." No response was had and no one came to the rescue.

On the return trip, while snowshoeing down one of the frozen lakes, Black Stone collapsed and died. His wife hauled his body off the ice and onto shore, where she buried him in the snow, wrapped in a rabbit-skin blanket.

Upon her return to the village, the flu had taken its toll and not many people were left. The surviving Indians moved to the Lac La Croix Indian Reservation and Kawa Bay was abandoned. Later, very likely after they had recovered from their ailments, Black Stone's friends from the La Croix Indian Reservation returned to the lake shore and built a grave house surrounded by a fence.

If a grave can be dug, items like a pipe, tobacco, or beads, are placed in the bottom of the opening with the body. In rocky country, this small house is put over the grave site to mark the resting place. The remains of the body have probably disintegrated by the time this is done.

Black Stone's grave house had a little door and a shelf inside with his pipe and his rosary beads (probably given to him by a Catholic Priest). "Canoe travelers" found this place and took the pipe and wampum — beads and sometimes shells used by the North American Indians for money. As time passed, the grave site disintegrated and fell apart.

Many years later, when I canoed down the river and into Kawa Bay on Kawnipi Lake, the old reservation site was still visible. I had the feeling that spirits still hovered there. The buildings had all vanished but the earth remained trodden and bare.

The Powell's have been in the Gunflint area for many generations, with roots that go back to their membership in the Lac La Croix Indian Band and with ties to Black Stone.

Betty's Great Grandpa, She-May-e-ane-unak (sunlight), was known as John Ottertail while working as a guide for the Canadian government in the Quetico Forest Reserve around the turn of the century. Her Great Grandma was Kaa-Kaa-Kee (raven). Ka-way-wi-gesi-kook, her great-great grandmother was the head of the family. This was customary among the Indians.

Betty's grandpa was Jack Powell, who was English and Irish. She remembers him saying he was born in Tawa City, Michigan. He never said how he happened to come to Ely. He married John Ottertail's daughter, Mary. Her Ojibwa name was Aquayweasheik and she was very proud of her heritage.

There is much written about the Ottertails, Blackstones and others who lived in that area in the 1800's to early 1900's. Detailed records are kept at French River, Canada.

Mary Ottertail, lived on Basswood, a Lac La Croix Indian Reservation in Ontario, Canada. She was 18 in 1901 when she married Jack Powell at Basswood Lake. At that time, he was employed on a logging train in the Ely area.

When Betty's grandparents married, her grandma was no longer, a member of the band because the tribe wouldn't accept her husband, who was a white man. Mary's grandpa, Tskee Kay Waw Sin (sunshine), told her he went to a meeting with all the Indians of the band. They made little wigwams on top of a hill. The medicine man was Mary's uncle. He got inside his wigwam to talk to the animals and ask them questions.

Jack Powell said, "He started pounding on his drum in that wigwam. Soon, the wigwam started to shake and dance! My hair stood on end. I was so scared, I did not understand their ways."

When the meeting was over, Mary was not considered a member of the band.

It was an unusual marriage, for Betty's grandma spoke only Ojibway and her grandpa spoke only English. However, they loved each other and somehow understood one another perfectly.

After a few years, Jack and Mary moved to Saganagons, where they raised five children, Frank, Bill, Mike, Esther and Tempest. Frank and Bill married sisters, Charlotte and Dorothy Bruneau, from Tower, Minnesota. They each built and successfully operated resorts on Saganaga Lake. Mike married Black Stone's granddaughter and guided and trapped. Esther married and moved to Port Arthur.

Betty s mother, Tempest, stayed at home. She trapped in the winter and guided in the summer. A single mother, she had three daughters, Betty, Janette and Minerva (who was several years younger). Betty missed having the presence of a father, but her mother told her it was often that way in those days — even as it is today.

Betty Powell told me the story of her Indian life and of learning to accept the newly arrived white man, while still trying to preserve her own heritage and beliefs. The history of Betty's family is a fascinating narrative of six generations of the Powell family, that begins with Betty's great-great grandmother, Ka-way-wi-gesi-kook, in the early 1800's and continues to the present.

The following is the story of Betty's life, as told by her in her own vernacular, recorded on tape. One is quickly drawn into Betty's world by the mystique of Indian storytelling. In writing down Betty's words, I have tried to preserve that essence.

In reality, Betty's story represents how the Indians lived, adapted to the white man's ways and survived in this north country sixty years ago. The central purpose of their lives was providing enough food not only for present needs, but to see them through the long winters.

BETTY APPEARS

I was born to a single parent over a half-century ago in a two-room log cabin built by my grandpa. One room was the bedroom with three beds; Grandma and Grandpa's, my mother's and Janette's and mine. Grandpa Powell got up every morning at daylight and made coffee. He served everyone in bed — adults and kids. The other room had a table, chairs, and a cook stove.

My grandma was my mom's midwife during my birth. It was at the northeastern end of Saganagons Lake, where I spent my childhood with my mom, sisters and grandparents. This vast wilderness would become my home, a home filled with love and respect for one another as well as for the land and all the nature that surrounded us. We were very poor. I didn't know that as a child. I felt rich because our home was full of love.

When I was six or seven years old, my grandma had a little rabbit snare line for me in back of the house. That was my job in the morning. I would get up first thing and go lift the snares. I'd bring home a rabbit and that would be our breakfast that day, shared by all.

Grandma would clean it and make a soup and that would be breakfast. It was usually about ten or eleven o'clock when we got the rabbit cleaned and cooked. We always ate just two meals; about ten or ten-thirty in the morning, and four in the afternoon.

There were snowshoe rabbits all over the woods then. They were large, with big ears and wide paws so they could travel on snow in the winter. In the late fall, they turned white and in summer they were brown.

Nothing was ever wasted. In the winter, when the hides were prime, they were stretched, dried and cut into strips. They were fastened end to end and woven into rabbit skin blankets. The blankets were impervious to the cold, even when sleeping out on the ground. Also, a small piece of the fresh hide could be formed around a person's foot and held in place with a stocking. As the hide dried, it followed the contour of the foot and became a very warm boot liner.

Betty's grandmother, Aquayweasheik (Mary Ottertail)

MOOSE CALLING AT TROUT LAKE - FILLING THE LARDER

I went with my grandpa and grandma and my mom to Trout Lake. It was a lake that I just loved, because we spent a lot of time there and it wasn't too far away from home. They were going to try to finish a cabin for that winter. I must have been about three years old at the time.

They had the cabin about half finished. Our tent was pitched outside while they were building the cabin. We could look out on the lake. It was so pretty there. The Cabin was built near a small river that bubbled along over a bed of rocks and small falls as it connected one lake to another. The white pine trees were large and protective. At a later time, it was the first cabin Janette, then nine, and myself, at twelve, were allowed to trap alone. It was a day's dog team trip from the farm.

On this trip, besides working on the cabin, my grandma decided we needed to get some moose meat to have for the fall. She would call in a moose with a moose horn. She and my mom used to call moose all the time. It was scary for me. They would call those moose and pretty soon, we would hear them answer, then we could hear them coming.

This time, we had a fire built by the lake and Grandma said, "I think I'll go down and see if I can call a moose." She went down there and called and called. Nothing answered her, so she decided we would just wait until tomorrow and see if we could get one then. We planned to stay there for several days. All of a sudden, we heard that old moose answer up on the hill. We heard it coming and my mom grabbed me and put me in the cabin. The cabin didn't have any windows in it. It was just built half-way up. She threw me down so the moose couldn't get me.

The dogs were barking and that old moose came down and kicked the fire. He was really mad. My grandma used to say, "Don't build a fire and keep it going all night, because when the bulls are in rut, they fight fires." I guess that's true, because years later, when Ken, my husband, was working at night at Taconite Harbor, moose would often challenge the lights on the taconite trains and be killed.

Hiding in the cabin, I could hear all this noise and thrashing around. I kept wanting to climb up so I could see what was going on, but the window hole was too high for me. Mom kept saying, "Where is my shotgun, where is my shotgun?" I finally climbed up high enough so I could see that moose stomping and bellowing and the dogs barking. They never did shoot the moose. I guess it got away.

After it was all over and everything sort of quieted down, we all got back to normal. We were scared, for the moose could have killed somebody. I heard my grandpa telling my grandma, "If you are going to hunt any moose or call any more moose, you go over on the other side of the lake so he doesn't destroy everything we have here."

Trout Lake had little trout in it. I don't think the fish were over one-and-a-half pounds. This area had never been logged so there were big pines all around. It was a beautiful little lake. There was a steep hill from Beaver River up to Trout Lake. Beaver River started at Singabits Lake, was the outlet of Trout Lake and eventually emptied into Saganagons. There were several beaver dams on the river where my grandparents and my mother trapped. They had fisher, otter and beaver traps all along that river in the fall and spring.

I remember the stories Grandma told me, about Grandpa and my mother trapping. The family was licensed to trap in the area. They "farmed" this area, never depleting the wildlife supply so there would always be "seed" left for the next and future years.

Each fall, my mother went with her dad to repair the four trapping cabins, located at least twenty-miles apart. They cut out the summer windfalls and re-distributed their traps to new locations so no area would be over trapped. The cabins were similar in construction and never required more than an ax to build. The logs were laid horizontal, with the corners cupped to hold them in place. The space between the logs was filled with moss, which had to be replaced or added to each year.

The cabins usually had two single bunks, a small air-tight stove and a table over which there was a small window. Nails were driven in many of the logs for hanging and drying coats and shirts. The roofs were covered with sheets of very enduring birch bark.

The birch bark had to be gathered in June. At that time of the year, the removal of the first, inner layer of bark on the birch tree left a scar, but it was free of any holes or blemishes and it did not kill the tree. It was this same bark, that could be folded to form a small basket, filled with water and placed over a fire to make a cup of tea. The two folds of the bark were held together by a partially split twig. This birch bark basket was made of the inner bark. It could stand a lot of heat and could boil water readily.

In preparing the cabins for a winter of trapping, it was also essential to have a stack of wood, that would last three of four nights, at each cabin. When trapping, or when checking the lines, any wood that was burned was replaced before leaving the cabin.

Sometimes, Grandpa and my mom would go for a week or two before coming back to get more supplies. The distance between the cabins was estimated by the fact it took four days, going real fast with the sled dogs, to check all the cabins.

The trapping cabins were compact and warm. They were never locked and could be used by canoe parties, in an emergency, when passing through in the summer. Then, food, blankets, snowshoes, traps or a gun could be left in a cabin, secure with the knowledge nothing would be taken. Now cabins are often broken into, even though securely locked, and stripped by traveling canoeists

Besides trapping, my mother guided fishermen in the summer. She worked so hard for her family. I can recall her carrying a heavy packsack full of traps when we would be on the trapline in the fall and early spring. It didn't seem to phase her as she was so strong. Then, in the summer, she carried heavy canoes, motors and packs over long portages. I can understand, now, why she was so crippled with arthritis when she got older.

In the summer, Grandpa would move the dogs out to an island. There they each had a house and were on a chain that was hooked to a cable tied to a tree. These *leashes* were long enough so the dogs could get to the water to drink. They ate boiled fish, thickened with cornmeal. We cooked it for them at home, then after it cooled, we took the canoe over and fed them. My mother, grandpa and grandma all used to carry 100-pound sacks of cornmeal over that two-and-a-half mile portage from Saganaga to Saganagons.

Mom was just the hardest working, kindest woman anyone could ever meet. She took good care of my sisters and me. There wasn't any problem I was afraid to go to her with — she always understood. I don't think I ever got a "licken" . . . not that I probably didn't need one! Instead, I just got a talking to. I respected Mom, and Grandma and Grandpa so much. I never back-talked them.

Betty's mother, Tempest, at Trout Lake cabin

HUNTING TRIP ALONE

I wanted to help supply meat too, so I did a hunting trip by myself. We had a double-barreled shotgun. One day, when I was about ten, I thought I was going hunting ducks. It must have been in the late summer or early fall.

Where we lived on Saganagons, there were three points of land. It was a neat place, for the ducks swam along the shore. I thought I'd just go over there and get us some ducks to eat.

I took the old double-barreled shotgun. I kept getting closer and closer. There were about five ducks lined up on this point. I thought this was going to be great. There would be all kinds of ducks for us to eat. Well, I pulled back and aimed, pulling both barrels at the same time. The gun gave a terrible kick and I went flying backward and hit the ground. There were ducks flapping all over. I was so proud.

I got four ducks. I hurried back to Grandma and I said, "I've got us some ducks."

She took one look at me and said, "We don't eat fish ducks (mergansers), but you are going to eat some."

I thought, "Oh, gosh. Now what's this?"

"Now you go down and pluck this duck," Grandma said, handing me one.

I went down to where we cooked for the dogs and it took me all afternoon to pluck the feathers.

I took it up and Grandma put it in a pail, salted it and boiled it. Oh, God, it stunk so bad. She said, "Well, you can have some of your kill." I tasted that stuff and I could just puke it tasted so awful, but she made me eat a couple of tastes.

She said, "Now I just want to teach you that you don't shoot anything that you don't eat because now you have wasted all those ducks." So I never shot another bunch of ducks unless I knew what I was shooting. But, I *was* proud when I was shooting those fish ducks. I thought I was a big hunter.

HUNTING TRIP WITH MY GRANDMA

My grandpa had given my grandma a .30 - .30 gun when they were married. She was the hunter of the family. My mom said when I was three years old, I used to go with my grandma and stand in the pack sack and then I would see things before she would.

As I got older, I often went hunting with my grandma. There was one time that I was really scared. There was a big bear that kept getting into our cabins over on Beaver Lake. There was a little river that came in from High Lake, where there were always a lots of suckers in the spring.

My grandma said, "I am going over tonight and wait for that bear. He will come in to eat the suckers." I said I wanted to go along and she said, "Well all right, but you will have to be quiet."

It was a dark night. Grandma carried the gun and portaged the canoe to Beaver Lake. I was always scared of meeting a bear on this trail. There were lots of big cedar trees where High Lake flowed into Beaver Lake. They almost looked like real people, standing motionless in the shadows.

Grandma set the canoe on the shore of Beaver lake. I guess I would have liked to have climbed in the canoe and gone back out on the water, but I wanted to go on this hunt with Grandma, so there I was. Anyhow, we sat by that river and we could hear the suckers jumping. It was in the spring, and there was quite a bit of water running.

As we sat there, Grandma poked me and said, "Be real quiet now. I can hear him coming."

The bear must have been in the middle of the river. He would reach down, get a hold of a sucker and throw it out on the bank. I guess he would go back later to eat them. I don't know, but that was the only way I could figure it out.

Anyway, the bear kept coming and I could hear him in the river. I was so scared. I kept telling Grandma, "Shoot him, shoot him."

She would say, "No, he is not close enough. I can't see him yet."

We had a flashlight, I guess, but she was just waiting in the dark until she could see him coming down this river. Finally, she cocked the gun and I knew she was going to shoot. She shot that old bear and I took off, but she grabbed me and hung on to me.

She hit him good and he just ran toward us. That bear came so close to landing right on top of us. He fell down and died in front of us.

Grandma said, "Well, we got him. Now we have to gut him. You hold the flashlight while I gut him out and we will leave him here over the night."

I held that old flashlight. I was shaking and I kept thinking, "This is the last hunt I am going on." I knew, of course, I would be at the next one. Anyhow, she gutted that old bear out and we left it there overnight.

The next day, Grandma and Grandpa went back. I don't know what they did with that bear. I don't know if we ate him or not. I know they sure didn't throw him away. We probably ate him. I know I didn't like bear meat. I don't think my grandma really cared for bear meat either, but she used to render out the fat from the bear and that is what we used for bug dope.

Grandma used to take this bear grease and rub it all over my head. I never had bug bites. My husband has since remarked I must have been a nice smelling little creature. I don't know how I smelled, but the bugs didn't bother me.

There were so many bear back then we just had to shoot them or they would have destroyed our cabins. They even tried to get in our home when we'd leave.

I recall another time, when we went hunting moose. It must have been in the summer. My Mom, Grandma, and my sister, Janette, and I were up Beaver River. We must have been short of meat and wanted to get a moose. I know they never shot a cow in the summer time; usually, it was a young bull.

Anyhow, we were traveling up Beaver River where we were camped. One night, it was pitch black again and my sister and I were in the middle of the canoe. As we were paddling up the river, we suddenly could hear a moose. It would dive and then it would come up and we could hear it.

We kept paddling and paddling. My heart was beating so fast, and Janette was younger than I and she was scared too. I was trying to hold her mouth shut so she wouldn't make a noise. Every time she was going to scream, I'd hold my hand over her mouth and almost cut her breath off.

We got closer and closer to this moose. It was diving and my grandma said, "No, it is a big cow and we can't shoot her." So, we went on and I don't recall we found a bull moose that night.

We must have gone back to the camp to sleep and I was scared all night with all the noise. It's a frightening thing when you can hear those moose diving. They come up and blow water out of their nose.

The second night we must have gone out again. It was the same thing. We heard a moose and kept paddling up closer and closer, and then I heard my mom say, "You better shoot."

We were getting awful close to it, but my grandma said, "No, I can't see it yet."

We kept getting closer and closer. We could almost touch the moose it was so close. It was a bull so my grandma smacked the water with a paddle and as the moose stepped up on shore, my grandma shot it.

We didn't know where we were, and the moose was coming almost at us. My mom started to back up the canoe. Grandma said, "No, don't. Just stay here. It's going to turn around and go the other way."

He did. We went ashore and the bugs were bad, so it must have been in the spring. Mom and Grandma found the moose and gutted it. We went back to our tent and stayed overnight.

The next day, Grandpa came over from Saganagons and helped get the moose out of there. I think at that time they had a canner, because my mom canned all night, trying to get this moose taken care of. We had meat then for the rest of the year.

Usually, when my grandparents got a moose, mom would cut it up and make jerky. It never spoiled because it was all dried and cooked. Weeks later, you could take this jerky, boil it up a little and it would get soft just like any meat. They dried the fish in the fall by hanging them up by the tail to dry.

Once Janette and I pulled a trick on my grandma and grandpa. We went down to the lake where we had a little dock that stuck out. It was really a neat place there. It was sheltered from all the winds and we had hills on two sides of us.

Those hills were my playgrounds. I used to go there and swing from tree to tree on the limbs. I just loved it up there. There were lots of squirrels.

From our home we could look out on the lake, and see many islands. We had some duck decoys. We took those old decoys and set them down by the dock. We thought we were going to pull a good trick on our grandparents. We said, "Grandma, there are a couple of ducks sitting out there."

She went out and said to Grandpa, "Oh, it's good ducks to eat." Then she went and got the shotgun and loaded it.

I am sure me and my sister were giggling and laughing to think we were going to pull a good trick on them. She shot and the decoys just came floating up. I could see the expression on her face. It hurt her when she shot, for the gun kicked her. She felt so bad that we had done that to her.

Grandma's arm was hurting for days from that old shotgun. We felt so bad and would never do it again. At that time, we just thought it a fun thing to do. We were so sorry we had caused our grandma to hurt.

THE BOUNTY OF THE WOODS

We always had net thread to sew with when we got back from camp. My grandpa said one of the best things the white man gave the Indian was net thread and then he told the Indians they couldn't net fish anymore. As a result, we always had a surplus of net thread to sew up anything that needed to be patched.

The birch tree was one of the better hard wood trees that we had. It was a very important product with many uses in our home. June is the month to get birch bark. Taking it at that time leaves a scar, but doesn't kill the trees. Grandma never took a lot of bark from one tree. It was used in the construction of canoes, teepees, wigwams, tickanoggins and baby sleepers.

Wa-pe-che-bi-zon were created and used by the baby for the first six months. A strip of birch bark the length of the baby was used to give the necessary back support. A little basket was filled with dried sphagnum moss. A blanket was laid under the birch strip and over the baby, whose hips were on top of the moss. This made a soft bed and the baby was never wet; the moss absorbed the moisture.

We could also make a little basket out of a piece of birch bark that had no blemishes. The ends were folded and held in place with a partially split twig. The little square basket was then filled with water and placed over an open fire. The boiling water made excellent tea.

Mother also made spoons out of birch bark, and birch bark horns for calling moose during rutting season.

I remember our trapping shacks had birch bark roofs on them when I was little. I think after Mom married Irv and they started trapping, they put tar paper on the roofs.

Birch bark was used for making envelopes. Once in a while, my Grandpa had to send a letter and he would make a birch bark envelope. My mom used to make designs on these envelopes, and that was real pretty too. Loose birch bark was used to start a fire.

We used to make slingshots out of birch crotches and an old piece of rubber. I don't know where my grandpa got the rubber, maybe from a tourist, but it was very precious and he never wasted it. We weren't allowed to shoot birds or anything with these slingshots. We just had them to shoot at marks.

The birch sap was used too. Grandma would cut a little slit and then poke a stick in the hole and the sap would run and drip into the hanging birch bark basket. When we would go or come from trapping, there would be sap in there. Grandma said that sap was very nutritional. It was, for you know the beaver eat birch and poplar. We would drink the sap instead of water.

Cedar was an important tree, too. It was very light, but strong. Rugs were woven from strips, an inch wide, from the inner cedar bark. To patch a hole in a canoe, a wide strip of cedar bark was applied with the pitch from a spruce, across the hole to make them almost waterproof. Cedar ribs were used with the construction of canoes. Cedar paddles were light and strong. Wooden strips of cedar were bent and used to protect the head of a child in a tickanoggin. They were also used to make baskets.

My grandpa used to make us little whistles from the aspen. In the spring, when it was easy to cut the bark off, he would cut a little tree and make us whistles out of it. My sister and I used to blow those whistles. Those were really neat.

He always made us bows and arrows out of an ash stick and fastened a string to it and a little stick for the arrow. We used to play we were Tonto or the Lone Ranger. Everything we had, like toys, were made from the woods. We seldom had anything that was bought.

Our dolls came from the roots of the water lilies. The roots were pulled up by the moose. They would float and we would collect them, dry them and whittle and shape them like a doll. We threw them back and forth when swimming.

Moccasins were made out of deerskin or moose hide. The hides were all tanned and I can remember my grandma and my mom standing alongside a fire to smoke-tan the hides. It was hot so this wasn't easy. Then my grandma would take these same hides and make a wigwam. It was made out of little poles and she would put the hides on there. Then she would get some poplar wood and would go inside and sit there and smoke those hides. It would be so smoky in there you could hardly breath. I remember, as a little girl I would crawl in there with her and lay down on the ground. I loved the smell of that smoked hide. I used to chew the hide like gum.

I liked to be near her and watch what she was doing. She would keep the fire going for a long time. She must have been so smoky smelling when she got out of there. I loved the smell of all those things. It was just a part of my life. That was where my moccasins came from.

I remember how neat it was to have rabbit skins. My mom used to put the rabbit skin on our feet and put a sock over it. The rabbit skin would dry and become a mold for our foot. We would have our own rabbit skins for our feet. We never had cold feet in the winter time like we do now.

My grandma made snowshoe rabbit blankets. She would weave strips of rabbit hide the size of a blanket. My grandpa had one and he said he could sleep anywhere, anytime and never be cold.

When we traveled, either by canoe in the summer or dog team in the winter, we always went as light as possible, with only the basic food supplies of tea, a bag of rice, sugar, salt and flour. Game was always abundant and available in the woods. There were partridge, snowshoe rabbits, porcupine, deer, moose, ducks, beaver, muskrats and fish available.

During the spring, there is a plant the Indians call cawtox. It grows along the water's edge in small, sandy or rocky bays. Cawtox looks like a tiny carrot with many roots. When we were paddling along the shore, if Grandma spotted cawtox, we would dig up the roots, wash them off in water and eat them. They were very tasty.

We used to occasionally pick mushrooms and eat them. Grandma didn't think they were the best for us. We didn't eat a lot of them — maybe just twice a year — once in the spring and once in the fall.

Because there are poisonous plants too, you really have to be careful and know what you are doing if you are going to live off the land. I always watched the squirrels and chipmunks to see what they ate.

When we caught a northern pike (a fish we ate a lot of) while on the trap line or just out paddling, Grandma would build a fire and let the coals burn down. Then she would dig a hole, put a few coals in it, lay the fish on them and add more coals on top. She would then put the dirt back in the holes and just let the fish cook.

When the northern was done, it was taken out and all the skin peeled off. We ate just the white meat. Gee, I remember how really good that was. We used to do all kinds of little things like that in the woods.

The porcupine was also important to us. It was a food source which we ate when we couldn't get anything else, or if we were on a trap line and ran out of food. Porcupine were very plentiful then. Grandma used to burn the quills off them over a fire and scrape their hide. Then we would cut it up and put it in a kettle to boil. When cooked, we would eat it and if I remember right, it tasted pretty good.

Porcupine is something we didn't eat a whole lot of, it was just for an emergency. My grandma always said it was the spirits come back in that porcupine that gave us the meat. It is a belief that sometimes, when out hunting a deer or a moose that runs right up and stands there, he is telling us that he is just giving us his meat because he knows we need to have it. That is kind of neat when you think of it.

My grandma got medicines out of the woods, too. We never had any of your modern medicine as I remember it. My grandma would go back in the woods and gather roots and stuff. I recall one time I cut my wrist and it bled so bad. She went back and got this long leaf — we called it adder leaf. She wrapped that thing around my wrist and it just stopped bleeding. The cut would clot whenever Grandma used adder leaf.

In the spring, the water is not the best; it is the run-off of everything. That is probably why we always had the stomach flu in the spring. That's why Grandma would get these herbs in the spring and boil them, so we wouldn't be sick to our stomach anymore. It was just neat all of the things they used just from the woods that we don't even think about. They never did tell or show us what herbs were used.

We used to chew the pitch on the spruce trees like gum. Grandma always said it was real good for your teeth. I don't think it helped my teeth, but she would tell us that. I don't think I liked it too well either. We patched the canoe with the pitch too, and used it for whichever came first, the teeth or the canoe. If we had a leak in the canoe, that came first.

Then another thing she used to do — if we got a terrible cold, she used to get a muskrat skin (the muskrats that live in the lakes and rivers). She had a skin that she kept specially for that. If we had a cold or something and our chest was congested, she would put that rat skin on our chest and then we would sweat, and she said that would pull all the sickness out of our body. I don't know if it did or not, but it seemed as if we got better.

Grandma used to go out in the woods when I would have my period and would be menstruating and have cramps. She used to boil up some kind of roots and I'd drink that and I just didn't have any more cramping. I wish I knew what that was today. Maybe when I ache with arthritis, I could take a little drink of it. It might help.

She used to get tea leaves from out of the swamps. She used to get leaves and boil that up, put a little sugar in it and it had a peppermint taste. Now you can buy this peppermint tea, and it is good for settling the stomach.

Grandma used to boil up a lot of things from the woods. If someone was sick, she would go back there and pick things. It was funny, she never took me with her. I wish now I would have gone with her, because I have asked my mom about it and she said she never knew, either, what all those herbs were for.

The trapping cabin on Big Lake

Janette and Betty - late 1930's

WILD RICE

My grandma, great grandma and my mom went down to pick wild rice on Whitefish Lake, Ontario. Uncle Mike and his family went too. We stopped at Gunflint Lodge and picked up some extra canoes from Justine. On our return we gave her some of the wild rice, that she was very fond of, for the use of the canoes.

The first time I met any of my grandma's family was at Whitefish Lake. We camped on a little point or island. At night we all got together, and we sat around the fire. It was the only time I heard my grandma sing and it was the first time I had heard drumming too.

My great grandma, Kaa-kaa-kee was going to give me an Indian name. She had to go to bed and sleep and dream a name. We were there for only a short time and I guess she didn't have time to dream an Indian name for me. That always bothered me. I wish I had an Indian name.

While we were down there picking rice I wore a pair of coveralls that buttoned up the front. I thought they were the greatest as I jumped out of them at night and jumped into them in the morning and started running. My mom said that is what I did a lot of — just running. I guess I'm still the same way. On the move all of the time.

They tried to leave me with my great great grandma while they were picking rice. I didn't want to stay with her. I was kind of scared of those people. They were so different from my grandma and I wasn't used to seeing other Indian people. My grandma and Mrs. Plummer and Mrs. Cook, from Gunflint, were the only real Indians I had ever seen. Grandma said, "All right. Get in the canoe." So I got in the middle of the canoe. They gathered rice all day. I guess the rice has shucks on it and when I got home that evening I itched so bad that I almost scratched myself to death. My grandma told me I should have stayed home. Being out there in that canoe was not very good.

Wild rice was a necessary staple that was harvested each year. The harvesting time was also a time when Indians came from Saganaga, Gunflint, Grand Marais, Grand Portage and Lac de Mille Lacs to catch up on the latest happenings.

After tapping the ripe rice in the canoe they brought the rice ashore where they spread it on a birch bark sheet and removed any small stems. They would then put small portions in a washtub placed at a forty five degree angle over an open fire. Rice could not be taken home green, for it would heat up, mildew and spoil. A short paddle, shaped like a canoe paddle, was used to lift the rice and let it sift back to the bottom. The heat and continual turning would loosen the husks. The rice was then put into a pit lined with cedar shakes on the sides and bottom. My mom would climb in and with a turning hip motion would grind the rice and that released the husks. My mom had some new moccasins made especially for this occasion.

Then the rice was divided into small baskets. My grandma and Mrs. Plummer would each flip the rice in the basket and the wind would carry off the chaff and leave the rice clean. They bagged all this rice and packed it back up the chain of lakes. We had many bags as it had to last us all year.

These yearly treks came to a sudden halt when the Canadian bureaucracy moved in with outside pickers and told the Indian families what portion of the lake each could harvest. The green rice was purchased from the Indians and hauled off to be mechanically husked, dried and sold. The gathering of wild rice by the Indians had been two fold. One for the winter supply for food and the other the joy of all being together again and learning of the recent marriages and deaths.

I would give anything if I could go back one more time and go wild ricing with all the relatives. I can only remember going on those trips a couple of times, when I was very young.

Betty Powell at her home overlooking the Baptism River

The Old Homestead — Saganagons Lake, Ontario

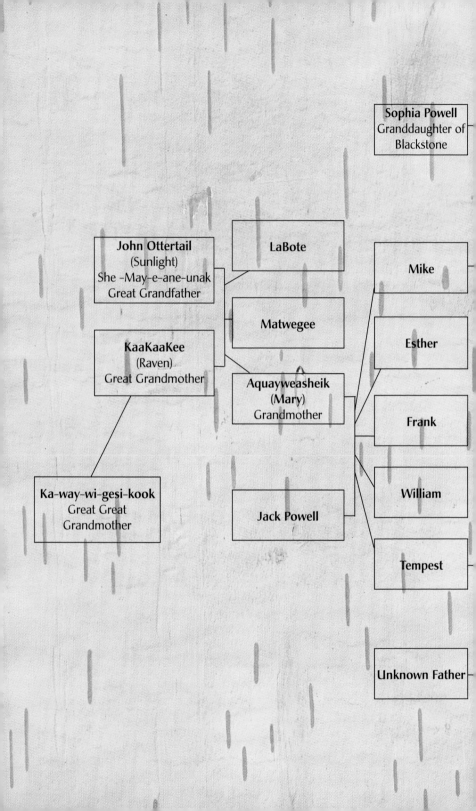

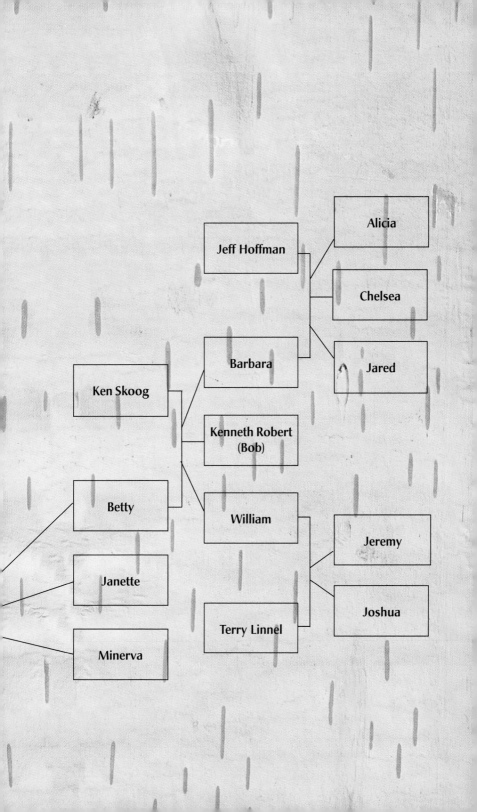

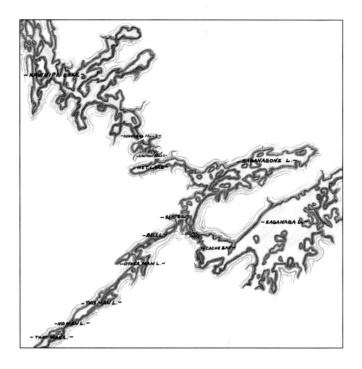

Betty's great grandmother, Kaa Kaa Kee

Betty's mother, Tempest - early 1950's

BLUEBERRIES

We usually went to Northern Light Lake to pick blueberries. There were lots of places where there had been forest fires and the blueberries were always plentiful after a burn.

First we had to make the long portage from Saganagons to Saganaga. Then we paddled to what later became known as the "Railroad Portage". This was the north route from Saganaga to Northern Light Lake. Sometimes, I believe we may have gone the south route across Saganaga, portaged around Northern Light Rapids, then about a mile up river, portaged again around Northern Light Falls.

Usually my uncles and aunts, Mrs. Plummer and sometimes Mrs. Cook were with us. Lillian Plummer came and, of course, my grandma, mom and my sister were always there. We camped on Northern Light Lake and picked berries. It was such a fun time because we were there with all the other kids to play and swim. You name it and we did it, but they made us pick berries too.

I recall Uncle Mike had this old, blind lady with him. It was his wife, Sophie's aunt, as I remember. She was always referred to as the old, blind lady. Mike and his wife Sophie brought her with them wherever they went. He used to carry her on his back up to the blueberry patch.

We went through a swamp and then up a long hill and carried all our stuff up there. Swings were made close together for the babies. They put up two ropes between the trees, fastened a blanket around them and took two sticks to hold the ropes apart which made swings. Separate ropes were attached to the swings. The old blind lady would sit where she could hold the ropes and swing the babies. That was her job while everyone else was picking berries. There were usually three or four swings involved. We would be up there all day long on an old burning.

There was a time we had to carry a gun with us because there were bear there. After my great grandma was attacked by a bear while she was picking blueberries, we were always aware of the danger. I can't remember seeing a bear there but my grandma always carried a gun anyhow.

One time we were picking berries when a fire started. It was two hills over. Every one was scared, and they said to pick up everything and head for the lake. They were worried the fire would catch up with us and burn us up. Mike went a running with that old blind lady on his back. When we all got down to the lake, they decided to move our camp out on an island. The fire didn't go anywhere. I guess it just went out.

The next day everyone went back up to the blueberry patch and continued picking. This was when Mrs. Plummer said she saw a muns-sa-tog-a-nah. No one seemed to know what it was, other than some kind of spirit, but they were really scared of it. At least my grandma and Mrs. Plummer were scared of it. They sat up all night waiting for it to appear but nothing came. I never did find out what it was.

When my mom and grandma got through picking berries, they had three of four fish boxes full. A fish box was usually made of Aspen, and would hold one hundred pounds of fish. It was used by Lake Superior commercial fishermen to pack and ship their fish to Duluth. My grandparents would carry all those berries across the long two and one half mile portage to Saganagons. When they got home they spent days and nights canning them before they would spoil. This was the fruit we had to carry us through the winter. It was the only fruit that I ever remember. They canned some and put them in the root cellar so they wouldn't freeze. Some blueberries were dried. These could be soaked in water when needed, and they would swell up and be like fresh berries. In spite of the work it was always a fun time for it was when a group of us would all get together and get better acquainted with each other.

Grandma and Grandpa Powell - Saganagons Lake, Ontario

SPRING PLANTING

We used to plant potatoes all over the islands in the spring. That used to be such an exciting time. We'd be gone sometimes for a couple of days. There was just Grandma and Grandpa and Janette and I, for Mom was guiding this time of year. We would go to these islands, and Grandma and Grandpa would dig up the ground and Janette and I would follow and plant the potatoes. We worked as fast as we could so we could explore the island and see what we could find. It was always great fun to do that for we would always have new territory to discover.

One evening Grandma said, "We have to get something to eat here. We haven't any meat."

Grandpa said, "When it gets evening we will go down in this bay."

That night we got into the canoe with Grandpa in the stern and Grandma in the bow. If we made any noise, we got a tap over the head with a paddle. We went down in that bay to hunt but didn't see anything. All of a sudden Grandma spotted a bear so she up and shot it. It was just getting dark. She wounded it. It was very seldom that Grandma just wounded an animal. She never liked to leave anything suffer in the woods. She said to my grandpa, "You better go with me and see if we can find him."

She told us kids to sit in the canoe, not to go anywhere and they took off in the woods. Janette and I were just sitting in the canoe getting more scared. It was getting dark. We could hear all kinds of things but couldn't go out on the lake because if they came back fast and there wasn't a canoe there they could really be in trouble.

I spotted a big birch that hung over a little river that ran into the bay. I said to Janette "Let's just go climb that tree." We could shinny up a tree faster than a squirrel.

We got out of the canoe and went over there and climbed up the tree. It leaned over the lake. We felt pretty safe then. When Grandma and Grandpa came back they couldn't see us in the canoe, but looked up and saw us in the tree. A bear is adept at climbing a tree, too. They were so mad at us for being up in that tree.

The next morning we went back to see if they could find the bear. As soon as they left we were out of the canoes and back up that big birch tree. They found the bear close to the water where it had died.

I was always scared of bear. I don't know why. Maybe it was because they made such terrible noises. They would rip up our cabins, smash the stoves and knock all the windows out. Sometimes the cabin was a total wreck.

PETS

The animals were my playmates when I was growing up. My grandma and grandpa always let us have wild things to tame if they were orphaned. I guess I tamed about everything there was to tame. I still can't understand how my grandpa, grandma, and mother put up with me. Anything that was orphaned, I took care of.

We had a little otter that I loved so much and I still think of him every time I see an otter track. He used to cuddle around my neck and dig in my pockets. He would go down and play in the little creek that ran close to our home. He would go to this little river to hunt and fish. Then he would come back into the house and dry off.

We also had a little beaver later on in my life. I have forgotten where we got this little beaver but I remember, just as plain as yesterday, when it used to live in the house with us. It was more like a cat because it never made a mess inside. She always made her wants known and went outside. Every time the wind blew she would try and plug up the holes that sometimes develop in a log cabin. She lived one whole winter with us but died in the spring. There was a doctor visiting us, and he did an autopsy. He thought she probably ate too much bannock and her digestive system failed to work properly.

Besides playing with our pets we did a lot of swimming. My grandpa never believed in swimming suits or exposing our bodies. I am still a little bit shy even now when I put on my swimming suit. Grandfather used to say, even if we wore shorts, "Go cover yourself up. Don't run around half naked." When we went swimming it was with long pants or long underwear. That's the way he believed, and that is the way we were brought up.

My sister and I swam in the lake shortly after the ice went out until in the fall when it really got cold. We would throw a set of rubber dolls into the lake and would dive for them. I guess we had Snow White and the Seven Dwarfs. I have little *Happy* yet. Sometimes, all day was spent diving and swimming. We threw our condamoo's back and forth (these were dolls made from the lily pad roots). We paddled in wash tubs, and we swam from island to island — until discovered and then curtailed, because it was considered too dangerous.

Later on, as pets, we had a bear and a moose. I remember the bear real well. One time when my grandpa came home from trapping he heard these little bear in a den. He looked in. The mother was dead so he brought these little bear home. He found them in the early spring — maybe in March. We fed them milk from a bottle. Then in the spring, they started to grow up and became very aggressive. I remember mostly the little bear we called Tuffy. He had a white face.

I had an old rag doll. It was not like dolls you see nowadays, for my grandma made all our dolls of flannel. Every thing I wore was made of flannel. I had this rag doll, and Tuffy used to get hold of me around the middle and give me a bear hug. I would hit him over the head with my doll and try to make him let loose. He wouldn't let go because he would want me to feed him something.

We had canned blueberries in the summer. That was the fruit we gathered and cooked the year before. They used to tell us not to feed any of the fruit to the bear. We understood why, as the blueberries had to be carried over the two and a half mile portage to get them home. We would take some fruit up on a hill, take a spoon along and Tuffy would always go with us. The other bear roamed around the house and never followed us like Tuffy did. We would go up on the side of the hill to eat blueberries. Tuffy would sit on a rock and start licking his chops. He was so glad because he knew he was going to be fed too.

As the bear cubs grew older, they became quite mischievous. I remember they would pull the tablecloth off the table when

Grandma would have it set. We knew their mischief would turn to violence the older they got. Somebody went down and called the forestry, and they came and got them.

Later we had a moose. My grandma and I were up behind the house at a little lake off the end of Saganagons. I don't remember the name but my grandma and I used to go up there trapping muskrats and beaver in the spring.

One time when we were back there, we ran into an old moose with a calf. This little calf wanted to follow us. Grandma kept telling me to just get behind a tree and stay there so the moose couldn't hit me with her hoof when she came by. Grandma had to shoot this old cow because she wouldn't let us get away. Grandma was so upset because they had to go and get the moose out for they never let anything go to waste. My grandma and grandpa and my mom had to carry that whole moose out over quite a long portage.

Grandma then went out on an island to dry the meat. She would lay it over some poles. Then she would build a fire with poplar underneath it and dry the meat very slowly, which would sometimes take two or three days. My grandpa would go to the island and help her dry the meat. My sister and I just loved that because we got to go too. We would run and play and find new things in the woods on this island.

Since my grandma had to shoot the old cow, we brought the little moose back home with us and fed it milk. This little moose stayed with us for over a year. I was a little scared of her as she got bigger because she got really mean. She tried to kick us with her front feet. If she saw us playing and didn't know what it was we were doing, she would surely take after us and try to kick us.

I remember my grandpa would be hoeing in the garden, and this little moose didn't like him doing that. She would lay back her ears and start chasing him. He dropped what he was doing and ran and jumped in the water.

As the moose got bigger, my mom got the idea, one day, that it would be good to hitch the moose up with the dog team and haul out some logs. She hitched the moose to a toboggan, along with the dogs and started out. The moose got panicky, kicked all of the dogs and wrecked the toboggan. That was the end of driving the moose.

Later on that summer she used to follow us wherever we went. We had a cabin down on Moose Bay, and she followed us along the shore. Mom and Grandma would always like to sneak away, but she would find them and follow them. We were hoping she would go off and find a bull and stay with him.

One time when they came back the moose wasn't with them. My grandma was real happy for she thought the calf had found a moose and had taken up residency somewhere else. That fall when they went to the trapping cabin to get it ready for winter they found her inside. She had gone in, and the door had closed behind her. She had broken her neck trying to get out. That was a sad thing and that was the end of our moose.

We had everything; chipmunks, partridge — or anything we could tame or that was homeless. We had ducks and seagulls. Grandpa almost called a halt on the seagull bit, as they wandered into the house and left their excrement all over the floor.

My sister and I had always had chipmunks for pets. The chipmunks almost drove Grandpa crazy. As they grew older, the few chipmunks produced an ever increasing number. Some of them would get in the root cellar and eat much of our stuff. Grandpa told us that was the end of that.

Then we had an owl. It was a big owl. We also had chickens at that time. As the owl grew up, it wanted to eat the chickens. My grandma would take a branch and switch it in its face to keep it away from the chickens.

The owl was neat but I didn't know what kind of an owl it was. It was very small when we first got it. As it grew older it used to go with us in the canoe. We were fishing all the time for the dogs. We had to feed the dogs in the summer time and that was one of the jobs assigned to Janette and me. It was easy for we loved to fish and would go over to a river not far from our house. There were so many northern there.

We didn't have rods. My grandma or grandpa would find a stick to which they attached some kind of a line. They put a hook on it and we dragged it behind the canoe. Before long we had plenty of fish. This little owl sat right on the canoe with us. He was supposed to be a night owl but everywhere we went he wanted to be there, too, to see what was going on. He loved it for when we would catch a fish we would always cut off a piece and give it to him. He would smack his little jaws, and he thought he was in seventh heaven. My sister and I used to spend hours over there fishing for the dogs and cooking for them. It was a lot of fun being born free and having so much area for our playground.

The owl grew up to be kind of a pest and a heartache for my grandma and grandpa. One night when it was late in the evening, and my grandpa went out to go to the toilet, I heard him hollering, "Jesus Christ, Old Woman (he always affectionately called my grandma Old Woman). The devil got me for sure." That owl had landed on top of Grandpa's head and dug his claws into his scalp. That was the last time I saw our owl. I think he took a little trip after that.

I never knew the English names of the birds. I only knew the Indian names, not only for these birds but for the ducks and the animals too. That was an oddity about my life, for my grandma spoke only Indian and my grandpa spoke only English. My mom, my sister and I spoke English but we understood Indian very well. Even today I have a hard time with the white man's names for all of these creatures.

LESSONS OF THE OUTSIDE WORLD

I never wore shoes in the summer. I ran barefoot most of the time. Once when I was playing with some visiting children from the guest cabin — one of the very few times that we would have other children to play with — they were laughing at me because I didn't have shoes and my feet were dirty. I am sure those children were running in the mud too, but they ridiculed me just the same.

I was so hurt that I ran back to my grandma and told her what had happened. She was angry with me and took me aside and sat me down. She said, "I do not want to hear you ever complaining again about not having shoes. How many people can feel Mother Earth underneath their feet all day long like you can?"

I walked away from there very proud and thinking all the good things I had. I loved the feel of the ground underneath my feet. I was sure the visiting kids wouldn't agree with me, but it didn't matter. Even today I love to run barefoot in the grass with Mother Earth under my feet.

I had another hurting time when we went to Grand Marais. My sister was in a tickanoggin and my grandma wore long skirts. We stayed at the Sterling Hotel on the shore of Lake Superior. That was the time when an Indian wasn't allowed in all the places.

Mrs. Sterling ran the hotel. She always had a room for anyone that came in from the woods whether they were trappers,

Indians or prospectors. She was strict, but all those that followed her rules were welcome.

My mother was out shopping and my grandma took me and my sister out for a little walk. There were kids on the street who were poking fun at me and at my grandma and calling her Indian, dirty Indian. It hurt me terrible.

They kept poking fun at my clothes. My clothes were made of flannel, and my moccasins were made of deer or moose hide. I was totally hurt and cried and cried. Finally my grandma took me back to the room and she tried to console me.

I will never forget what she told me that day. I thought, as a little kid, that I just wanted to go home where I was safe and people didn't hurt me. She said, "That is just the way life is and you have to learn to live with it. You are Indian and you should be proud of that. Don't you ever do what those kids are doing to you. You always look inside a person."

I still do that today. I hate it when I hear on TV where people are knocking one another because of color or different clothes. I just don't feel that God would ever want it that way. It is hard for me. I am very emotional to even talk about these things that are hurting.

That pain was a good hurt for it taught me a lot. My grandma was a great teacher for she told me never to be like that. I hope and pray to God that I never am. I know I never will be.

I remember taking a trip to McKecknie's Mill, which was located on a lake now called Round Table Lake on the route to Fort William, Ontario. My grandma and my mom, my sister and I made this trip by canoe. We left Saganagons and went to Saganaga, then down the border lakes to Gunflint. When we got there we stayed a couple of nights and visited with Mrs. Plummer and Mrs. Cook. It was a good time for them as they all spoke Chippewa and they had a good time visiting.

Mrs. Plummer always made up a big kettle of soup. We all ate and had a good visit. Mrs. Plummer, Lillian, George and Charlie Cook, and some other children, joined us. It took us about a week to go down the border lakes. If there was a wind or something we would have to lay over for a day. Both the children and adults used to love that because we could swim and visit with everybody. It was a lot of fun for us for we got to see other people. Then we took off and headed for McKecknie's Mill.

Along the way, we stopped and visited with the Bishops, who lived on North lake. We had a good time there, too, for that was the first time I can ever remember eating popcorn. When I was a kid my grandma always popped the wild rice. We ate it just like cereal today but we didn't put anything on it. I really liked this new popcorn.

When we got down to McKecknie's Mill I heard my grandma speak English for the first time. She sometimes spoke a word or two but never entire conversations. McKecknies had some little cabins, and they had a farm. They had turkeys, geese, big ducks and chickens. These old turkeys were very mean, and they chased me. I was just petrified of the turkeys. I had never seen anything like that before. I sure didn't like those birds.

Anyway, Grandma went up to get us a cabin. She came back and told us they had a cabin for us. We went over to this supposed cabin. It was a chicken coop with chicken droppings all over the floor. My grandma was so mad and said, "Just because we are Indians we don't want to sleep in a place like this." She went back up there and I am sure she must have talked English because she was really mad. Anyway, she came back and they gave us a couple of nice cabins on Round Lake.

That was where we took the bus into Fort William and Port Arthur, the towns that are now combined as Thunder Bay. That bus was not the best either. It was a shaky old thing. I don't know if it came every day, but it would come in and take us to Thunder Bay. This was a fun time, too, because sometimes we would get to go to a show and go out and eat in a restaurant, and we stayed in a hotel. That was just a fun trip

Another time we went over to Gunflint. There was a couple by the name of Ben and Mama Gallagher. They had such a beautiful log cabin on top of a little rise on an island. They really liked my mom and my grandma because we would go over to Gunflint every once in a while and visit.

I remember my mom and grandma said before we got there — and I am sure my sister was along too — "If they offer you anything to eat, you just eat it and be polite."

I thought, "Okay," but I was getting a little scared, wondering what I might have to eat. They asked, "Does your daughter like bananas?"

My mom said "Oh, I think so."

They gave me this banana. I didn't like it but I ate it anyway. After I ate it Mr. Gallagher said, "Oh she must have liked it, shall we give her another one?" I was hoping my mom would say, "No. that's enough," but she didn't.

They gave me another one. I ate half of that banana and it made me sick and I went outside and had to throw up. I remember hoping they would think that because I went outside and puked this all up that I wouldn't need another one. They didn't give me any more but even today it is hard for me to eat a banana.

On the island they had a pond, and in the pond I think they had some kind of little animals. I would go down on the rock and watch those little things. I thought that was the most beautiful place. I would like to go back there again and see that place. I haven't been there for many, many years. I have been to Gunflint by road but you don't really see anything but a little part of the lake.

There were many good times, but we had to have the bad with the good. I often think about that when we look out at nature, here at my home located in the *Outside World,* where we live on top of a hill near a little river. I see all the beauty around me and I think, "You know, if it didn't rain we would never appreciate the sun."

This is true because we look constantly for the good things in life and never accept the bad, but that is what makes the good things good.

The only times of my life that I remember hurting was when other people couldn't accept me for what I am. There is so much of how much money you have, what kind of a car you are driving, all of which means a lot to some people. I'm perfectly happy with what I have. That is what I was always taught.

JANETTE AND I STARTED TRAPPING

My sister and I started trapping in the winter when I was about twelve and she was nine. Janette and I had three dogs in our team that we drove all the time. I don't know why, but they used to fight a lot.

We started once from Saganagons, going toward Beaver Lake. It was the Beaver Lake portage where I used to be so scared of bear. I was halfway over that portage and the dogs got into a fight. We always carried a stick along to swat the dogs when they fought. They could kill each other if we didn't get them apart.

I hollered at my sister to help me with these dogs. I looked back and there she was up a tree. I was so mad at her. I said for her to come down and help me but she wasn't going to come down until it was all over.

After the dogs quit fighting and we got ourselves straightened out, she came down and said, "If I'd been alone and the dogs started fighting, I'd have climbed up the tree and just stayed there."

My mom had the dogs she drove well trained. She would drive up to a cabin and tell those dogs to lie down, and they would stay right there while she was in the cabin.

A little dog named Tippy was the lead dog. When the trails were visible, Mom would go down the lakes directing the dogs by calling gee for right and haw for left. When Mom couldn't see the trails at all on a wind blown lake, Tippy felt for those trails and never faltered. Tippy was one of the greatest leaders I can remember.

In the spring when we got those terrible storms we really depended on our dogs to take us where we wanted to go. It would snow real hard, then clear up and then snow again. My grandma called it the Push Keesh. It was like a white out. Little Tippy would feel out the trail and know where to go.

The dogs all knew where the cabins were. When they got to a trap they would just stop and lie down and chew the snow balls off their feet. Then wait until you lifted the trap and reset it if we had anything. The dogs were surely our survival. I don't know what we would have done without them. I just loved all our dogs.

My mom used to make the dogs canvas moccasins in the spring. The ice would get so rough it would cut their feet without that protection. We had an old sewing machine she used to make the moccasins. Grandma made all our clothes on it too. It was the treadle type. Mother used to take that canvas and cut it, sew it, and fasten it around the dog's feet. They always tried to step high in them but it was the only way to keep their feet from getting hurt.

My grandpa and my mom told us about Grandpa having a team — half of them were wolves and half were dogs. The wolves made good sled "dogs" but they were scared of everything. Sometimes when Grandpa would go some place and the team would see someone coming or see something across the lake they would turn around and run miles back before they could be stopped. He never had to worry about the dogs fighting with another team, anyhow.

We had lots of sled dogs. That was our way of getting around in the winter time. When we used to have the dogs — the old female would have pups. I'd crawl in the doghouse and lay with her and those little pups. I remember the smell of their breath. I loved to hug them. I often think of that, now.

We were really afraid to do a lot of things and we talked to Grandma and Grandpa about many of them, but we had to make our decisions finally. I guess they thought we were very qualified, because we started taking care of ourselves and going with them on the trap line with dogs when we were very young.

My sister and I would start out with our dogs, a small amount of food and our traps. We'd go up to our trapping grounds at Big Lake for a couple of days and get ourselves organized. There was a lot of fur back then. Then we would go on up to Greenwood. That, too, was a beautiful lake. We'd set our little mink traps. There were tracks every place we went; lots of moose and deer tracks, wolf, fox, and fisher. Now this area is all clear cut, which just makes me sick.

I never cared to kill anything. I grew up not a very good trapper. I trapped because I had to. It was a case of survival. I used to cry when I would get something in a trap and had to kill it. My grandma was a good teacher. She said "You always want to think that chicken and that turkey and cow wants to live, just as much as these wild animals, so just look at it as a source of food." I still do that, for I still hunt deer but that doesn't mean that I ever liked to kill anything. I'd rather take a picture of it or watch it than to kill it. I feel real close to the animal world.

One time in the spring, my sister and I had our dog team and traps ready and my grandpa told us, "I wish you kids wouldn't go, because I think the weather is going to change to rain and the lakes will turn to slush." We went anyway. We stayed at Big Lake, Greenwood, and then we were going to go over to Burnt Lake. We started through that country and about halfway through one of our dogs got sick. She really got sick and we just didn't know what to do. We decided we couldn't take her with us, and we didn't want to kill her.

After building a lean-to for a shelter and cutting wood all afternoon, we decided to stay with her and made camp for the night. We just had our axes and a little crosscut saw that Grandpa made and that we carried with us. There was just enough food to get to Burnt Lake, and then we were going home from there. Luckily, we got a beaver so we had something for the dogs and were sure they could make it the next day.

Anyhow, Janette and I built a fire and sat under this lean-to. We were both scared and really didn't know what to do. That little dog suffered so and we tried to console her and comfort her. About one a clock in the morning she died. We thought she may have swallowed a bone or something.

By then it was too late to start out. It started to rain, and the lakes turned into slush. About three o'clock in the morning we ran out of wood. We were cold and it was still raining. We just didn't know if we were going to make it back this next day.

When it began to get daylight we got our stuff together and started out. The two dogs weren't strong enough to haul our sled anymore so we just had to take our pack sacks. We had to take off our snowshoes and just wallow through the slush. It was almost up to our knees. It was really bad.

We made it to Burnt Lake, and decided we had better not wait there for things to get worse but just to go on home. We started wading down through those lakes. Halfway from Burnt Lake to Saganagons we were so cold it was necessary to stop and build a fire, warm up and get dry. We did have our little tea bag and sugar and stuff with us. We built a fire on the side of the lake and dried our socks out. We had been taught how to survive.

The dogs were exhausted, too, for we had to leave their harness on them. We didn't dare leave the harness up there at the lake because some animal would come along and chew them up. Those harness were very precious to us for my mother hand made all the harness and collars for the dogs. We brought out the harness from the other dog too.

We got our socks fairly dried out and our feet warm and a cup of hot tea in our belly, and then felt like we could make it the rest of the way. It was the worst slush I had ever walked in in all my life.

We got into Saganagons after dark. It was late, probably six or seven at night. Grandma and Grandpa were so glad to see us. Of course, they didn't know all this had happened. They thought we were just holed up in a cabin some place. That is what we usually did — just stay in the cabin until the weather got better. We just had too many problems that time to hole up.

That was an experience that was real trying. Knowing how to do things is what makes the difference in freezing to death and dying of exposure out there. We had many of those experiences, where we had to make decisions on how to handle things.

When we told them what had happened my mom said that we will just wait until this slush freezes and then we would go up and get the sled. In a couple of days she hitched up her dogs and we all went up there and got the sled and brought it back. We buried our little dog up there in the snow bank. Janette said we had to make a little cross for her so we went and got a little pole and tied the sticks together with a string.

I remember, later, as we went by that place, I would always go over there and see if that little stick was still there. It was there for a couple of years and then it vanished. That dog was such a nice little dog.

We loved all our dogs. They were just like a part of us. They were what took us from one point to another. They were our best companions and would never leave us no matter what.

Betty and Janette with beaver from the trapline

On the trapline

A CLOSE CALL

One year when my sister and I were on the trap line we went to Trout Lake. We'd usually drive our dog team, but this time the ice was real weak. Trout Lake wasn't too far from home but it would take almost a day because we had to go along the shore since the rivers and lakes weren't safe.

My mom said, "I wish you wouldn't go. It is early yet and you could fall in the lake."

We wanted to get our traps out while it was good going, without too much snow. We packed our little pack sacks, carried our snowshoes and away we went.

We used the cabin at Trout Lake that was built when I was about three and Grandma called a moose. Now it was Janette's and my favorite place to go. We set out most of our traps going to the lake. We got to Trout Lake real late that night. We had bunks supported with poles and piled high with hay for our bedding. We went up there in the summer and grandpa would cut hay with an old scythe. He would put fresh hay in every cabin so it would be good for the winter.

That hay really felt good to sleep on. We had just a little, light blanket that we carried along. We couldn't leave it in the cabin because the mice would chew holes in it. So we built a fire and cooked up something, it was probably tea. No wonder I was so scrawny as a kid. We ate, but not always good things.

The next morning when we got up it was a beautiful morning. The ice had seized up real well so you could walk along the shore. We were sitting there drinking tea and all of a sudden, I saw something out of the corner of my eye. My grandma had taught me to see anything that moved. I said to Janette that there was a fox coming along the shore. Janette grabbed the gun and went out the door.

The gun went bang, bang, bang! I hollered, "Don't shoot! We can't get it if it falls out on the lake."

She never heard me at all but just kept shooting. She never did hit the fox. It ran across the lake and along the other side. I was glad when she missed it for if the fox had dropped out on the lake, I would have had a hard time keeping her from going after that fox and drowning herself. I really respected the lakes with thin ice.

We went back in the cabin and I said, "You should never have shot at that fox." We looked out the window and there came my mom, walking right along the shore where Janette had been shooting at the fox. I had a cold feeling that ran all through my body to think we could have killed her.

Mom came over to us and said, "What are you shooting at?"

Janette was just shaking. She said, "Mom we didn't know you were coming."

Mom said, "Well, I really got worried last night thinking you might have gone up here and fallen in the lake and maybe frozen to death. This morning, before daylight, I started tracking you and just figured I would come up and spend a day with you, then we could all go back together."

We set out the rest of our little traps that day. She stayed overnight with us. We had a great time visiting and talking about everything. We always had such a good time together. I can't ever remember my sister and I fighting about anything. We had to get along pretty good or we wouldn't have had anybody to talk to.

Some days on the trap line we decided we would talk nothing but Indian. We wanted to learn to talk like my grandma. In the morning we would agree that we would talk only Indian. Boy, by about noon we had to start talking English. We were trying to remember Indian words and couldn't remember them. We finally would give up and just start to laugh. We could say a lot of words but to make a conversation was not so easy as we didn't know some words and couldn't tie everything together.

Tempest holding a lynx cat

SHOOTING RAPIDS

Janette and I were a few years older with more trapping experience when we canoed over to Beaver Lake and on to Little Long Lake. All of the lakes have different names now.

We went down there in the spring of the year to trap beaver and muskrats. It was a day's trip. We always had a tent with us in case the wind came up and we couldn't make it paddling up Saganagons.

We had a pretty good catch that day. We came to the rapids where a river ran down into Saganagons. There was a quarter or half mile portage there. Janette said, "Gee I'm so tired. Lets not carry all this stuff over the portage. Let's run the rapids."

I thought "Oh boy." I was scared we might dump with all this stuff, but we decided to take the chance.

I was in the bow, and she was in the stern. The water was really running that day because it was high, as it always is in the spring, so we had some really good rapids to go over.

Anyway, we got about halfway down, hit a rock, spun around, and tipped over. The water was cold that time of year and running fast. I went under the water hit my head on a rock, and finally bounced up and got over on the shore. I probably wasn't under water very long but it did *seem* a long time.

I was so scared. I didn't know where Janette was and I didn't know where the canoe was. I started hollering for Janette. I couldn't see anything — our pack sacks, our beaver or anything. Everything was gone. Finally, I got enough strength and courage to get up and run along the shore. I saw Janette on the shore at the bottom of the rapids trying to catch the canoe and all the stuff that was coming.

She said, "Betty, are you all right?"

I answered, "Yeah, I'm Okay." I told her to grab the canoe, for without that we couldn't go anyplace. Grandma and Mom wouldn't come looking for us until the next day because they knew we might be gone another night. Janette got the canoe, and we got ashore.

We were cold and soaking wet. Our pack sacks were floating out there in the lake. So we got in the canoe and paddled to a little island a short way from the rapids. We went out there and rescued all our pack sacks and whatever we could get. I remember I had my little .22, my favorite gun as a little kid. That was tied to the canoe as a precautionary measure. Usually, we never did that when traveling, but there is always a risk when shooting a rapids.

We decided we had better stay on this little island and dry everything out. We never bought tents — we always used one of the little tents our grandma made. They were small and light and she waterproofed them with something. It happened to be a nice day so we dried out everything. It was probably three or four in the afternoon by then. It wasn't cold, but a nice spring day.

We rescued most of our beaver and muskrat — some of them floated and some of them sank. We finally went to bed. Along about the middle of the night we heard the dishes rattling. I woke Janette and she said it was a bear and grabbed the gun and crawled outside. I said, "What are you doing?" and she said, "It must be a bear."

It turned out it was only a muskrat or a mouse. That was probably two in the morning, and we didn't sleep much after that. We were just laying there, waiting for something to come and were imagining all kinds of things.

We didn't run anymore rapids after that. Not when I was along anyhow. I could just imagine hitting rocks and drowning out there. That was a good lesson. Even though it is always tempting to run a rapids, instead of being lazy we took the portage.

SPRINGING OUT

Every Spring, about the middle of April, we used to go on our last trapping trip. We called this "springing out." I used to love these times. Grandpa used to go over to Beaver Lake and down Beaver River a few days before the rest of us. We always used to spring out down there.

Spring is so beautiful. The sun is always warm during the day and would warm our bodies. Not like trapping in the winter. I recall those times we would be on the trapline and it would be so cold — sometimes twenty below zero or even colder.

I used to think, when I was a kid, "I'm not going to do this all my life, I'll tell you." My hands would get so cold, trying to set traps. Worse yet, was lifting the traps when there was something in them, especially under-water sets for beaver and otter. Sometimes, I think that's why my mom had arthritis so bad, from being in all that ice water so much of the time.

Springing out wasn't so cold. Overhead the geese would be flying north and the partridge would be drumming. There were all kinds of animals, beaver and muskrats.

My grandpa would go over to Beaver Lake first and make us a camp alongside the river. He'd make a shelter out of balsam boughs but we took along a tent and sometimes an airtight stove. We'd haul the canoes over by dog team and we all stayed two or three weeks until the ice went out, camping along the river. The whole family literally moved there for two or three weeks while we trapped.

The ice on the river was starting to go out that time of the year, so when we got to the rotting ice, we would load everybody into the canoes, unhook the dogs and pole the canoes along like a sled until the ice gave way, then we paddled to the nearest shore. Our dogs would swim, when necessary, or run along the shore to follow us to our camp.

That was where we used to get much of our fur. Janette and I used to love that for it was all new territory for us to explore. We would go up Beaver River with the canoe, and there would always be animals swimming.

Grandpa used to be camp cook. He would stay at the camp and cut wood all day just to keep the fires going. Grandma and Mom were the trappers. Janette and I trapped mostly muskrats when we were little because they were easy to catch.

One year I had quite a fright. Early one morning we were on Saganagons when I fell through one of those slush holes where the water bubbles up. My hips slipped through it and my mom couldn't pull me out. God, I almost froze to death. She had to chisel around and around to get me out of there. I was careful to never get in one of those holes again. I didn't see it but just slipped into it.

Except for that one time, I always enjoyed springing out. We had lots to eat for we just lived off the bounty of the woods. There was no other way for us to survive. We had to live off the land. You couldn't survive by trapping nowadays. Things have changed so much, even in the relatively short time I have lived.

OUR RELIGION

The following historical insights were recorded by Oberholtzer of Rainy Lake:

Priests had been trying for a hundred years or more to Christianize the Indians in this north flowing watershed. So the Catholics were determined to make a big drive and in the winter sent out notices to all the Ojibwa tribes in northern Minnesota and north west Ontario, living along the old fur trade route and speaking the same dialect, inviting them to a big powwow up on Shebandowan Lake.

They came, but remained adamant. They had their own worship and it was ancient. Each day for three days a different priest spoke. The Indians listened and then they presented their own orator, Black Stone, who answered every one of these men ending finally with a reminder that the Bible and the Birch Bark Scrolls both came from God and one is for the white man and one is for the Indians.

Whenever you ask how it happened that the Indians never joined the Christian church, the answer is, "Because we had Black Stone."

My grandpa was English and Irish. He was Catholic, but never talked much about religion. I think he had some bad experiences when he was young. When his mom died his aunt took care of him. When his aunt died, all the belongings were left to the Catholic Church. They were supposed to take care of Grandpa, but when he was about thirteen years old, they just turned him out on his own. He lost everything so he didn't talk too much about it.

My grandma's religion was the Indian religion. She taught me her religion as a child. Her religion was the earth and that is what God gave us. Her god consisted of many spirits — the god of the wind, the god of the rain, the god of the sun — all were the god of the earth.

She always talked about a God, the head one above us all. She said He gave us this earth and gave it to us to care for. If you abuse it, you aren't going to live on it very long. Whatever comes from Mother Earth is part of us.

My grandparents always watched the wolf and the eagle and they learned from them because they were very smart. The animals were like their friends and their relatives. That is why I love animals for they are really my best friends. I love to watch them.

Grandma used to tell me that the stream running by our little house was part of God. He made that water run so all the little animals could live, and we could drink out of it. If you just watch you can see God everywhere. It is very hard for me to hunt now. I said before that I always like to watch things instead of killing them. Grandma told me we have to kill to survive. That is just the way it is. She always told me if you watch those animals you will be able to hunt well to survive in the wilderness.

I don't belong to any church. I am not really sure which church I would belong to. I don't believe in the baptism if only those who are baptized are saved. My grandpa was baptized but my grandma was not. So I guess when I die, I hope my spirit goes wherever Grandma's spirit is.

I just figure she lived a really good life and probably never set foot in a church. I can't see anything wrong with her religion. It was all about this earth. Take care of this old earth and it will take care of you. You destroy it, and it will destroy you.

I guess that is the way I still believe too. We really had religion in our home — a different kind of religion, perhaps, but to me a very good religion. We never fought over it but just respected everything around us. We never tried to force others to believe our religion. As I look out of our window, here, and I see things going to pot on this earth and people throwing garbage every place, I can surely see things going down hill. Hopefully, we will have enough sense to turn it around.

We learned about the white man's Christmas and Easter, not from its significance in their religion, not by a priest, but by contact with the wives of Uncle Bill and Uncle Frank. To us it was just a time of giving and sharing. It had nothing to do with a god person.

The Ojibwa in Grand Portage and Grand Marais were influenced more by the activities of the local Catholic priest. The Indians living on Gunflint Lake would sometimes receive a yearly visit from a priest whose doctrine they politely listened to but informed him they had their religion which they preferred.

At Gunflint, Justine's mother had a big dinner on Christmas day for her Indian neighbors. In some parts of the world it would be called a Christmas dinner. Here it was just considered a yearly get together. This was followed by an afternoon of stud poker with matches used in place of money. I think these Indians learned to play poker with money from the crews that built the P.D. railroad across the lake. (P.D stood for Port Arthur, Duluth and Western but was known locally as Poverty, Want and Distress) I'm afraid hard cash was the stakes used at that time.

On Saganagons we were still more remote. A priest came to our place by plane once. Grandpa met him with a gun. We were never bothered again. There was a time when the Canadian government made an attempt to take the youngsters from the wilderness and put them in a catholic boarding school in Port Arthur-Fort William. There they would be taught to read and write. My grandpa wasn't going to let anyone take his grandchildren away. He met those planes with a gun too. Janette and I used to run and hide when we heard a plane come in for fear someone was after us.

There were no more encounters with the priests and the Canadian government eventually offered a self teaching course if it was desired. It could not be understood by the Indians, but Charolete and Dorothy, who married my uncles Frank and Billy Powell, used it to teach their children.

I never had any formal schooling, other than the correspondence courses from the government. My grandpa tried his best to help me with them, but he had only a third grade education and really didn't believe much in school. He was sure I'd grow up to be a trapper the rest of my life and live in the woods.

I'm glad they didn't send me out to a boarding school. I wouldn't have had the love and support only parents and grandparents can give. I would have missed out on all the things that we did. There wasn't a day that went by that I didn't learn something about nature. A lot of that can't be learned from a book.

As long as I can remember, we always had a Christmas and an Easter. We never brought the tree in until Christmas Eve because there just wasn't room enough in our house with Christmas stuff. We didn't have ornaments as we have now. We took pieces of catalogue and with flour and water we made little ringlets. That is what we trimmed our tree with. We thought it was beautiful.

It was on a Christmas Eve, when I was quite young, that my mother had ordered dolls for Janette and myself. It was the first bought doll that I would have. She waited and waited. She had to go to Gunflint to get the mail. The package never came.

The day before Christmas she told my grandma that she was going to Gunflint to see if that order had come in so the girls could have their dolls for Christmas. My grandma and grandpa begged her not to go because the weather was bad and the ice condition wasn't that good either. She said, "No, I'll be careful."

So away she went, and I can remember my grandma and grandpa walking the floor that night wondering if she would make it. Along about four or five in the morning she got home. She said, "Well I got the order and the kids got their Christmas dolls."

She said it was really tough going. It was sixteen miles to Gunflint following the lake route so it must have been a long trip in the night with the dogs. She had to snowshoe some places as she wasn't too sure of the ice. She wanted to be sure the ice was safe to walk on. I will never forget that. That was a great thing for Mother to do. Mother had a bit of Grandpa's temper but she had a whole lot of my grandma's kindness.

STORYTELLING

I just loved to sit and listen to some of the stories my grandparents used to tell us. Nobody wrote down the legends and stories we heard as children. They were passed on verbally and now many of those tales are lost forever. Grandpa told us stories about when he and Grandma were first married. It is hard for me to remember those stories now, for they go back an awfully long time and I was just a little girl when I heard them. That is why I began to save the stories that I remember on a tape recorder. Those recordings were the basis for this book.

Grandma always told stories about the wolf. The Indian stories were always about wolves. She used to tell us about old Chevee. This was to teach you not to be selfish. Chevee killed this big deer and he was going to share it with all the other wolves. He figured when night came he would just go over there and take a lot of the meat and hide it under his pillow. Then he'd have this meat after they had cleaned up the deer.

The next morning he woke up and reached for the meat under his pillow. When he examined it, he found it had all turned to sticks. If you do not share with others the meat you have taken for yourself, it will turn into wood or stone or something.

Another story Grandma used to tell was about the dancing spirits. Northern lights were very sacred to my grandma. She called them Death Dance of the Spirits. When she used to see them in the sky, we would all go out and watch them. She said, "That might be some of your ancestors dancing."

One time, beyond midnight, the northern lights dropped to the earth like a curtain swallowing up everything in its undulating folds. I remember how beautiful it used to be when we saw the northern lights dancing around in the sky and sometimes they would even be in color. Sometimes you could even hear them. I think I could anyway.

I don't recall seeing northern lights now like I used to see them. Maybe I'm not up at the right time. I wish I had asked my grandma a little more on how that legend came. When you are young, you just take every thing as it is and never ask a whole lot of questions.

Grandma used to tell me stories about the family too. I remember one all about bringing a cow and a bull to the farm.

My grandpa wanted to provide the best home he could for his growing family. He called his place a "wilderness farm." There was a big garden, where he grew rutabagas, cabbage, carrots and potatoes. He had chickens and a goat, too. When Grandpa decided he needed a cow and a bull for the farm, the closest place to purchase them was at Winton, near Ely. He and my Uncles, Mike and Frank, constructed a sturdy raft on which he built a strong corral.

He tied two poles, for and aft, across two canoes spaced well apart, much like a pontoon boat. He put the cow into the corral on the raft, which had been fastened across the top of the canoes; one regular canoe and one square stern canoe with a small outboard motor. He moved slowly and precariously down the lake to the first portage.

The cow was unloaded and tied to a tree. Grandpa and the boys then went back and got the bull. They unloaded the bull at the portage and put a collar on him, to which were attached two ropes. These ropes were fastened to the raft, which was detached from the canoes. With the cow following, the bull pulled the raft across the portage while Mike and Frank portaged the canoes. This tedious procedure was repeated on each of the ten portages it took to safely reach the farm.

That bull added a new dimension to everyone's lives. In this wilderness, everything that was accomplished required physical labor. Dogs were used in the winter for travel and hauling supplies. It seemed quite logical that Mike, Frank and Bill, who were dragging big, heavy logs for the construction of a new building at the farm, would think of something to make the job easier.

Because the bull wasn't doing anything but standing around, Mike got the idea that he could use the bull to skid the logs up to the cabin. He tied a log to the bull, using the collar and ropes my grandpa had fashioned for portaging the raft. The first trip to the cabin site went quite well, with the bull behaving peaceably. The second trip, however, was a catastrophe.

Something startled the bull, causing him to get very upset. He started bellowing and running, with the log bouncing wildly behind him. The cow was standing beside the hill. The log spun around, missing the cow's legs by about four inches. Finally, the bull went down to the lake and ran in the water. He jumped out and ran back through the garden with the big log knocking everything down.

Grandpa was beside himself, yelling and hollering, "Stop that bull from ruining the garden!" Great Grandmother, Kaa-Kaa-Kee, lived up on the hill a little ways. Mom said she could hear her shouting, "Shay Hih! Shay Hih!" She tried to hide so she could get in the house so the old bull wouldn't run her down.

The bull turned and ran for the barn. Mike was so happy when he got that bull stopped.

Another time, Grandma told me, Uncle Bill and my mother went over to a creek, to a spot where they cut hay for the cattle. Somehow, they got that old bull mad and he started chasing them. Mom ran up onto the haystack and grabbed the pole that extends upright through the center to hold the hay in place. Bill stayed on the ground, opposite from the bull.

Mom was hanging onto that pole and every time the bull rammed the haystack, she would go flying up in the air. She was laughing and thought it was great fun. She never considered she might have been killed if she had slid off the haystack. Fortunately, the bull tired of the chase and my mother and Bill were able to escape back across the creek.

Betty's grandparents and uncles, Frank and Bill, rafting supplies

Uncle Frank rafting the bull

GRANDFATHER WAS PSYCHIC

My grandpa was a very psychic person. We were very close to nature back there. Everything I was taught was from the woods or from the animals. They went by what the lake looked like or what this animal did or that animal did, by what the weather was going to be like. If the loon would get up and fly and holler early in the morning it was going to blow. So they would never get up and go paddling that day. It would blow if they did. My husband sometimes thinks I'm goofy, but we still go by some of those ways of life I was taught.

My grandpa always dreamed. His old aunt would come to him in his dreams. His father was killed in war. I think it was the Civil War. His mother died and his aunt raised him. My youngest sister, Minerva, was named for that aunt.

I don't have a lot of stories about my sister Minerva because I never really got to know her when she was growing up. She was quite a few years younger, and I was already out working when she was a kid. After my mother and Irv were married, Minerva moved to Thuder Bay, then to Port Authur to live with my Aunt Esther. Then she married and moved to London Ontario. It wasn't until our mother was hospitalized in Duluth, and Minerva and I spent fourteen days together there, that I got a chance to really know her. I never realized how much alike we were until then. We have been very close ever since.

Anyhow, my grandpa knew everything we did before we did it. We never did a whole lot of things that were bad because he would surely know about it.

I recall one time my Uncle Bill built a cabin over on Saganagons. It was a beautiful cabin made out of logs. My mom had the key to it because there were people that would stay there and go fishing. They would hire my mom as a guide. When they left she would clean the cabin. Sometimes my sister and I went over there with her. We later took the key from my mom, and we thought we were going to take some of their towels and then we would pay those people for them after we got some money, but it was really stealing.

Anyway we went over there, and we took those towels and cached them on top of a hill where we lived. We planned that when we built our cabin we would have some nice towels.

Well, I'll tell you, grandpa went to bed and the next morning he got me out of bed by the ear, and my sister too, and said "What have you kids been into?"

We denied everything. "I know you went over there and took some towels or you took something out of that cabin."

We were petrified and, finally, he made us tell him what we did. He made us take him up there on the hill and take those towels and put them back in the cabin. Then when the people came back he made us go over there and tell them what we did. That was one of the best lessons I ever learned.

That was the way my grandpa was. He knew when someone was coming. He could put his hand on the table and make it just dance. He must have had a lot of powers. I was very frightened of those powers until I grew older. I now have a little of those powers, too, as do Janette and Minerva. It seems to tell us what is going on or what is happening.

My children don't like it too well when I know what they are going to do. I grew up with that feeling real strong and never dared do anything as a child because I knew my grandpa would know about it. I don't think my grandma had anything like that because I never heard her talk about it.

JANETTE AND I BUILD OUR CABIN

Janette was about nine and I was about twelve. We both played instruments. I played the guitar and harmonica and she played the mandolin. It just got to be too noisy for my grandpa and grandma in that little two-room cabin we had, so we decided we would build our own cabin.

We had such beautiful trees on a hill behind our home there at Saganagons. That's where we cut down our trees. We decided we could haul our logs out with our two dogs. Janette discovered that we could go faster down hill, riding on the log. With one end placed on the toboggan, and both of us on the log, the dogs ran as fast as they could to keep from being run over. Grandpa saw us whiz to the cabin site and called a halt. It was too dangerous.

An old ax, a cross cut saw and a draw knife were our tools. We peeled the logs with the draw knife, then we decided how big the cabin was going to be. I think it was determined by how big the logs were. It ended up about sixteen by twenty, or maybe a little smaller than that. We never believed in measuring anything. We just cut the logs and notched them out and put them up.

This was a big task for us. We were busy every day. I have pictures of us up there, notching the logs for the cabin. The worst part was when we had to roll them up on top of the cabin. That was really hard for us. I remember my grandpa and grandma used to come out once in a while to help us get those logs up there.

We got pretty good at making the notches in the logs so they would fit together. Once in a while my Uncle Bill would give us a few pointers on how to do it. We got that old cabin up by spring. We never believed in a level. We just went by eye. It was a three-room cabin — a little kitchen, a bedroom, and a living room.

In April, we hauled all our roofing logs over to Uncle Bill's on the snow-crust. At this time of year the snow on the trails and the ice on the lakes thaws a little with the heat of the sun. During the night it gets colder and they freeze forming a hard crust. This makes for excellent travel. It becomes soft again by ten or eleven in the morning making travel very difficult.

Uncle Bill had a saw mill and he told us he would saw the logs for us. We went about six or seven miles up and down hills over these three little portages, taking one log at a time with the dog team and dropping them off at Uncle Bill's. He sawed them into roof boards for us. Then we hauled all the lumber home.

We had to get up really early, before it would get daylight, to get over to Uncle Bill's place, pile a light load of lumber on the toboggan and then haul it back. We could make two or three trips in one morning before it got too soft. We finally got all our lumber back.

We got the roof on the cabin, and it was really starting to take shape. I remember how proud Janette and I were when we saw the roof on this cabin. Then we got some tar paper and put on top of that and we were all set. We had to wait until the snow was gone before we could chink up our cabin with moss. We put in the windows and we had our own little cabin then. We enjoyed that.

We found out building a cabin wasn't as easy as it looked but we never gave up and we finished it. We even had closets in there. I can never remember having closets in our home. We just hung our stuff on nails or poles stuck into the logs.

We used to sit in our cabin and play our guitars, sing, and stay up as late as we wanted. We enjoyed that. We had to buy our own kerosene because if we stayed up late we were responsible for that. We even took a few groceries over there because we liked cooking once in a while. I guess we just wanted to be independent.

The next fall we decided we had to have a stove, beds, and tables. I think we built our own tables. We bought a little cast iron cook stove. I wish I had it today. It wasn't a very big one but it had an oven on it and four or five lids on top. We had a little airtight stove for heat. We had to save our money to buy all that stuff. I think that was when we went to Grand Marais and bought ourselves some nice towels.

That little cabin still stands and Irv uses it as a trapping cabin. I would just love to go back and visit that little place.

The cabin Betty and Janette built

Betty and Janette building cabin - Minerva standing in front

Janette and Betty posing in front of their cabin

AN INTRODUCTION TO THE OUTSIDE

The summer after we had finished our cabin, I started working at Jock and Ida Richardson's resort where I was suddenly thrust into a different world. They lived in a house boat next to their resort on the Canadian side of Saganaga Lake. I wanted to earn some money so they gave me a job. I don't remember how much I was paid. I know it was just enough to start buying a few nice clothes.

I lived in the house boat too, for Ida said fourteen years old was too young to be in a cabin alone. I helped wash dishes and do anything there was to be done. About once every three weeks I'd get lonesome and have to go home for several days and then I would go back and be all right again.

Jock and Ida used to have a lot of parties and he used to sing songs. I always liked being around people so that part wasn't hard for me. It was harder for me to leave Janette, for we had been together so much and did everything together. She was too young yet to go out and work. When I'd leave and go to work, I would miss her because we could talk over things that was bothering us. When I was away from home I didn't have her to talk to.

The next summer I worked at Chick Wauk lodge for Lydia and Art Nunstedt. Their resort was located on Saganaga Lake at the end of the Gunflint Trail. They didn't have certain jobs that you were responsible for like they do now. Then, we would get up early in the morning, wait tables, go clean cabins, then wait on tables for lunch, and go back and clean cabins, then come back and wait on tables for supper. We'd be there all day until nine or ten at night or until we got our work done.

I remember Lydia was very strict with me to be sure that I would be in my cabin at a certain time and making sure I didn't go out with boys. She was worried about me getting into trouble.

This was good as I wasn't used to being out by myself and not knowing about the dangers of being a young girl. My mom and grandpa and grandma never taught much about that part of growing up. I didn't know you had to learn all this yourself. All about sex and everything. Now days they have it advertised on the radio and taught in schools.

It was a little different for me back there in that other world. You did not talk about those things. That was a hush subject. So I was glad I worked for people like Jock and Ida and Lydia and Art because they took pretty good care of me.

When I was about fifteen, Janette and I decided we were going to go to Fort William and Port Arthur and start work there. We thought we would go to work in the winter instead of trapping. We were getting tired of trapping. We saw some ads in the paper, and we went and applied.

Janette applied at Cooper's. He was the fellow that used to buy our fur. I applied at Muriel and Mitch Lozowy's. They needed someone to take care of their children. So we went over there and applied and each got the job.

I was to start in a week to take care of their kids. Janette got a job as housekeeper for Cooper's wife. We came back home and got our stuff. I remember how sad it was because our mom and grandma and grandpa just hated to see us go and figured we would really get into trouble when we got out there. We all cried a little bit as we left home but we were determined to do our thing.

Muriel and Mitch Lozowy were like second parents to me. They were just wonderful people. I had to learn so much. I wonder now how anyone so young could ever fit into a world so different. They were so good to me and helped me in so many ways. Of course, I loved their children.

Muriel's mom lived with them then. She made me dress up every time I went to town. I would have to put heels on and a dress. I never had to dress like that before. I thought I would rather have my little britches on, the way I dressed up there in my jeans, but here she always made me dress up nice when I went downtown. It taught me that to be in the outside world you had to look neat. I had long braids then. They told me to cut my hair and they got a permanent for me. I was really IT.

They had an older son. I used to love to go to the picture show. I had never gone to shows and stuff like that, and they would never let me go alone. They made their son go with me, and he really hated that. He wouldn't walk on the same side of the street with me or sit near me in the show, but he knew he had to be responsible for me. He made sure to do that because he knew he would get in trouble if he didn't.

Janette and I would meet someplace every day. We wanted to go to dances at night so we talked Muriel and Mitch into letting us go to the dances (the Coopers weren't so strict with Janette). We both loved to dance. We'd go and dance until twelve, and then have to take a taxi home. Janette would get off the taxi first because she was closer than I was. I had to tell Muriel where we were going and exactly what time I would be home and she would be up waiting for me.

The next day I would have to tell her what we did, how the dance was and everything. They were neat people and are still very important in my life. That was a very good time in my life because it taught me a little bit how to fit into the outside world. I could have gotten into trouble if I didn't have someone to guide me.

I would have to take the bus every month because I would get lonesome to see Grandma and Grandpa. Once, at the border, I got out of the bus and went to the bathroom and left my purse in there. I went back and my purse was gone. I lost all my money. I felt so bad but, of course there was nothing I could do because it was gone. I had gotten paid thirty dollars for a month besides my room and board. Thirty dollars was a lot of money for me. I was going to buy Grandma and Grandpa something when I got to Grand Marais.

I got to Grand Marais, and I had to hitch a ride up the Gunflint Trail with the mail bus. Don Brazell was the carrier and he would let us ride with him once in a while. Then I told Mom and Grandma and Grandpa what had happened. They consoled me and told me they would give me enough money so I could get back. I had a bus ticket to get back to Thunder Bay.

Janette didn't last too long. She worked two months and then she quit. I stuck it out and worked there for six months. I came back home for the summer because I could earn much more money as a waitress with tips . That was my first time in being out in a city and being away from home. It was all quite an experience as I look back on it now. It was fun and yet scary. I just didn't know how to fit in, coming from the background that I had, but I made it anyway.

The hardest thing about being away from home and working for other people, was I trusted everybody. When I started going with boys, they would tell me they would have me home by a certain time then once we got out there they did not want to bring me back. I don't remember the liquor but the guys with me would be drinking beer. I just hated beer. I never drank when I was a young girl. I never even thought of it. We never had beer or liquor at home. I guess seeing people drunk made me sad. I just couldn't imagine anyone acting like this and falling around or saying bad words. My grandma never swore. The Indian people don't have swear words in their language. My grandpa used a few of them but my mom never did.

I learned very fast in the outside world I couldn't trust anybody. If they said they were going to do something, that did not mean that they really would. It made me want to go back to that other world many times, where I felt safe.

Where I came from we had to trust people. We never had any reason not to trust each other. I lived in such a small little world. All of the people that were around were my relatives. We all trusted each other.

When I started working in the outside world — that is where school became so important. Previously I had said I thought the learning in the woods outweighed school. I didn't mean a person shouldn't go to school. When you work in this other world you learn school is necessary. Taking part in all the activities they have in school helps you to get along with other people and other children. Anytime when I was younger and had any trouble with other children I would run back home where I would feel safe in the woods.

KEN SKOOG AND I MARRY

The next summer I worked for Al Hedstrom at End-Of-The Trail Lodge located on Saganaga lake at the end of the Gunflint Trail. Kenny Skoog, a Grand Marais boy, was working as a dock boy to begin with, and I was working as a waitress, cabin girl, and wherever they needed me. I recall the first time I met Kenny. He was very handsome and I thought to myself that I really liked him. We started going together, and I didn't get so lonesome to go home after that.

I thought, "This man really likes the same things I do." He loved the woods and he loved hunting and that was similar to the same things I did. By fall we were married. That was when we started our life together.

I taught him quite a bit about the woods. I remember one time he was guiding and he caught some fish and he came running up to the kitchen and he said, "You better come down and help me. I just don't know if I know how to clean these big fish."

I went down there and showed him how I was taught to clean them and helped him a little bit. Now he can clean fish much faster than I can. It is strange how when we start out learning from someone else how good we can become by just trying.

The night we got married was in October. We were up at his mother's and dad's farm. We didn't want, nor could we afford a lavish wedding, so we were married by Judge James Creech in Grand Marais. We had twenty five dollars to our name. Kenny tried to give the judge some money for marrying us, but Judge Creech realized we didn't have much money and he said for us not to give him anything. We didn't have a car either, so we took a taxi — back up to Ken's folk's place. Then we had to get someone to take us back up the Trail.

The next day we took this twenty-five dollars and went back to town. There was a hardware store and we bought a spring and a mattress and a few pots and pans. Then we headed back up to Saganaga.

It was snowing and blowing and the worst weather you could ever imagine. I'll always remember the anniversary because of that terrible storm we had in October. So we didn't start out with a bang, but I was perfectly happy.

We had cut some logs and bought a little piece of land. We planned to start a little resort. That was our dream and our plans. We had built a little cabin on a sand beach. That is where we spent the first winter. We had a roof over our head and a little cook stove. We had it made! Ken's mother gave us some sheets and a blanket. What more could you ask for? We weren't worried about the food we would be needing. We were just going to be trappers and live off the land.

That first winter we about starved to death. I was trapping, and pregnant with my daughter Barbara. I'd go on the trap line trying to make a little bit of money to live on. That was a very tough winter. One time all we had to eat was beaver meat. I didn't like beaver meat and neither did Ken. Here came my sister with the dog team and she had some moose. We threw the beaver out to the dogs, and we had a feast on moose meat.

We really lived on moose meat most of the time. That wasn't hard for me because I was used to it. I am sure it was hard on Kenny because he wasn't used to it.

We had three little dogs then too. They were Scottie, Chief and Bambi. That spring we decided we would go "spring out." I was as big as a house so we decided we would go to Saganagons where my grandma and grandpa lived. My mom didn't live there anymore (after marrying Irv). She and Irv were going to "spring out," too.

I remember my mom saying to me, "I just don't want to see you go off there in the woods when you are pregnant."

Mom and Irv went up to Greenwood or Burnt Lake. She said she worried the whole time until she came back and saw I was still alive.

I didn't know when the baby was due — approximately June, July, somewhere around in there. That's no problem because I drove dogs all winter and never worried about being pregnant. That seemed the least of my problems.

We skidded the canoe on the ice. Scottie was ahead pulling the canoe, and I was walking alongside and so was Kenny. My mom was sure that was the last time she was going to see her daughter alive. She was sure I was going to die some place, having that baby and falling through the ice. She could just imagine all kinds of things.

Kenny had to have his Cheerio oats. The way we were brought up, Cheerio oats was the farthest thing from our minds to take along on a trap line because then you had to have milk and all the other stuff.

We went down to Beaver Lake and camped in a little tent. I guess we caught a few muskrats, a few beaver. It wasn't too much that we caught anyhow. As soon as the ice went out, we came back to Saganagons. We cleaned our muskrats out, and I tried to tell Kenny how we put them on a board and why we put a little stick up the middle of the board. That way, when the hide dried we could easily pull the stick out which then gave it some slack to pull the board free.

He said no that wasn't the way he was taught. He knew how to stretch all these muskrats. When it came time to take them off the board, they wouldn't come off. There we were tugging on these darn muskrats and trying to take them off the board. If only he had listened to me. Lots of times he didn't want to take my advice because he wanted to prove that he knew how to do all these things.

I remember the first time we went out and he started building a fire — he did it like the Boy Scouts. I'm not saying anything about the Boy Scouts. I never saw a boy scout fire, that is just the way I was told.

Kenny always liked to carry a little fuel oil. We don't carry fuel oil on a trap line. We use birch bark and twigs and I said, "Kenny let me start the fire." No he was going to be the fireman. He is getting better starting the fire now but he still carries the fuel oil along with him. I still don't agree with the fuel oil jug.

I recall one time that winter we went up to Greenwood Lake. Kenny always had a lot of back trouble. We went up to Greenwood, and he got sick up there. I mean, *he really got sick*. He couldn't even get out of bed. His back was bad and we only had enough food for two or three days. It was up to me to cut wood and try and get some food for us before we ran out, and I was pregnant then.

So I cut a tree down and hauled it into the cabin. We had this old crosscut saw. It was hard to saw by myself. I'd haul a log into the cabin, and then Kenny would crawl out of bed and help me saw it up.

Then I went out and set rabbit snares and caught some rabbits and made a soup out of them. It wasn't his favorite meal but I think he was just tickled pink to have any kind of food. We spent about four or five days longer than we planned.

My mom wanted to come looking for us all the time but I felt we were grown up now and didn't need anyone checking on us and had told her not to come. I was sure wishing I could see my mom's face coming to check on me because I just couldn't handle this problem.

I don't know why I didn't start home and get some help. I guess I was scared Ken couldn't do anything by himself. He couldn't get out of bed to take care of the fire. We had those little air tights, and the fire didn't last too long. He'd be building a fire all the time.

Finally, he got well enough so he could start home. There was lots of snow and hard going. We came down through Beaver River. The river was not good, and we shouldn't have been walking on it. He couldn't walk in the woods, and I couldn't break trail for him being pregnant — it was too hard for me. He told me many times he just wanted to go out and sink himself in that river. He hurt so bad and couldn't walk, and it was just lucky that I had some background in the woods. We finally made it home to Saganagons, and he just lay there three or four days. He just couldn't get going. He has had back trouble all his life so it wasn't anything new I guess.

I recall one of our first Thanksgivings together. I think it was the second year. We had a little radio and heard on the radio it was going to be Thanksgiving. Thanksgiving had little meaning to us. Living in a remote area demands another set of rules. The days are not kept track of on a piece of paper. Time is hooked up with events — *the baby was born the year of the big storm* — *we had a light harvest the year it was so hot and dry.* As a result, many Indians have no knowledge, even, of the year of their birth, let alone lesser dates.

Anyhow, I said to Kenny we should go out and see if we can get a partridge so we can have Thanksgiving. He took the little .22 and away he went. He chased around that woods trying to get one little partridge for Thanksgiving.

He got one and I cooked it up and we thought we had the world by the tail — we had partridge for Thanksgiving. I don't know what else we had with it. About a week later we listened to the radio and discovered we had celebrated Thanksgiving a week too early. It was going to be the following Thursday. Kenny said, "Well, forget it. I'm not going to tramp around in that snow and get another partridge for Thanksgiving."

We had a lot of good days back there, then. We didn't worry about anything, and there wasn't really a whole lot of stress. We were happy and I guess that goes to prove you don't need a whole lot. It's just your state of mind that makes you happy.

The next year we started to build our big cabin down near Currans Bay. We poured the forms and started making plans to build a two bedroom, living room and kitchen. It was a beautiful cabin when we finished it. It is down near Currans Bay now. I thought it was a mansion. We worked all summer on that. He was guiding then at Chick Wauk Lodge.

Ken and Betty in their first modern home in Tofte, Minnesota

BIRTHING BARBARA

That spring I had Barbara. I flew out to Thunder Bay and stayed with my friends, Muriel and Mitch Lozowy. I didn't know exactly when the baby was coming. I didn't have any doctor follow-ups or anything like that. We didn't have insurance and we didn't even think of that stuff — in our family, the babies were always born at home.

I remember the story about the time my Uncle Mike's wife, Sophie, was going to have a baby. Mom said she would be there when it was time for the delivery. Because she lived ten miles from Mike, he was going to start his outboard motor in a washtub of water when labor began. That was Mom's signal to come. Outboard's did not have mufflers to quiet their motors then. That loud, low noise would carry for many miles in the quiet wilderness.

Art Smith, a guide, stopped by for a visit and was told when he got to Saganagons to tell Tempest Powell to come, that the birthing was soon. Art got distracted when he met another fellow en route, and forgot to deliver the message. The time came, and there was no sign of Mom.

Mike ran his outboard motor propped up in the tub of water until all the water splashed out and the motor seized up. Mom never heard a thing from her cabin on Saganagons, but Charlotte, Mike's sister-in-law, did hear the motor and responded by running nearly five miles. By the time Charlotte reached the house she had chest pains from running so fast in the cold air. She was crying, she hurt so bad. Mike couldn't stop her. She was worse than the baby.

So there I was in Thunder Bay with my friend, Muriel, waiting to have my first baby. I stayed out there for about three weeks. It was a long time waiting for this baby to arrive. Finally the baby was going to come, and Muriel got a hold of Ken somehow. He came to Ft. William one night to see the baby. I had a real tough time with this delivery and it was just a good thing I didn't have her back on the trap line, because I don't think I ever would have survived.

I remember when I got in this labor room — nobody ever told me what birth was about. I had seen dogs have pups and stuff like that, and I never heard dogs hollering and screaming, like in this labor room. The women were hollering and screaming, and I thought, "Oh man, this has got to be the end. I'm going to die here."

I had a real nice doctor. He was Muriel's doctor (Muriel was the woman I previously worked for). His name was McCloud. I laid in labor for about thirty-six hours. The doctor said, "You can holler. It is good for you."

I thought, "I'm not going to scream and holler like that — that would be the worst," and I don't think I ever did, either.

The baby couldn't be born so they put me out and took the baby by forceps. Anyhow, she was born and she had a sort of big head. Her head was kind of twisted from the instruments they used to deliver her.

The next morning when Kenny came in, the nurse came and told me my husband was there. Barbara looked so much like her dad that they knew he was the baby's father right away. He came in to see me, and I wanted to go home so bad. I just didn't want to stay there any longer, but I couldn't leave. I was in the hospital for about ten days.

After that, I stayed with Muriel for a little while. She was a very good seamstress, and she'd made Barbara the most beautiful little dress for me to bring her out of the hospital. I took her out to Muriel's and she made such a fuss over her because she loved babies.

I stayed there for about four days, and I couldn't stand it any longer. I called Kenny and got a hold of him somehow, even though he was out guiding. I told him I was coming home and was going to fly in a Seabee. These are planes that didn't land on floats but just on the belly parts. After we landed and I got home — the next time that plane landed the belly broke open, and if I had been on it with Barbara, I am sure we would both have drowned, so we were very fortunate. I've been lucky all my life. Things have always worked out.

Mom said Irv had been in the plane on the next trip when the belly collapsed. Mom was standing on the Customs' dock when the plane landed and it just sank. She thought that was the end of Irv. He got out somehow so it was real lucky that time.

We flew into Saganaga, and I was so glad to see our little home. We were still living in that little, tiny home. It seemed just a mansion when I got there. I had to do all my washing by hand. The first year I didn't have a washing machine but had to use a tub and a washboard. I did all my washing like that.

I guess it turned out to be one of the loneliest summers I ever put in there. Kenny guided such long hours. He got up at four in the morning and went down to the landing to get his boats ready. We only had the one canoe, a square stern with a little motor on it, and we didn't have any other boat so I didn't have a way of getting anyplace. I was just lonely on that sandy beach with a tiny baby, and I used to worry how I could get out if anything happened. It was really kind of tough there then. To fill my time I used to try and work on our cabin and dreaming how it would look when finished.

Once Kenny took some fishermen up to Northern Light lake, and they stayed there for ten days. Boy, I was so lonely. Mike Deschampe, an Indian neighbor whose wife had died, would stop and see me once in a while. He was always real good to us. My mom would get down once in a while but she was busy guiding then, too. Everyone was busy in the summer time because that was the time they made their living. My Uncle Bill would get down once in a while but very seldom did I have company.

I was always scared at night of bear because we did have bear around the house. We had our dogs, and they would bark if something came. I just remember it as being such a lonely time.

I didn't eat very well that summer. Barbara and I both got sick, and we went out to Grand Marais. We were really sick from lack of nutrition, and it wasn't because we didn't have the food. It was because we were lonely. I didn't really know how to take care of a baby. It's really strange how when you are young and you have a baby it is just instinct on how to take care of them. I guess my instincts weren't the best that summer. We didn't have all this canned baby food nor these disposable diapers either.

I made it out that summer, and the following fall we moved to Grand Marais and Kenny went to work there. We moved into Grand Marais and rented a little cabin there. We had running water and everything so that was really kind of nice.

It was a big change for me. It almost broke us the first month we moved down. There was a co-op store in Grand Marais. I was used to buying groceries every six months, or even once a year. All of a sudden I had access to a store every day, and I'd go down there and buy all this nice stuff like strawberries and ice cream. Oh man, it was just great. But when the first bill came by the end of the month, Kenny just about had a nervous breakdown. We owed so much money we couldn't charge any more and we lived pretty slim until we got that bill paid off.

That was the end of my big spending. I had to learn real fast to conserve and save money and I did, too, once I got out and learned how you had to do it when you lived in the outside world.

I remember how excited I was when I'd get in these grocery stores and there would be so many neat things. Not being used to buying all that stuff, it was just exciting to me. It's hard when you live back in the woods like that and then move out into a different world and take on all those responsibilities. I had lots to learn.

A RUN TO CATCH BOB

We moved back up to Saganaga in the spring and Grand Marais in the fall. For several years, Kenny and I moved back and forth so he could work each winter. There was no more of this trapping for now you couldn't make a living at it.

First he drove a pulp truck for his uncle, then after a couple of years he went to work for Consolidated Water Power and Paper Company. Eventually, he got permanent employment at Erie Mining Company in 1957.

I couldn't trap anyway, with Barbara to take care of and being pregnant again. I wanted a son and my grandma said, "I think you are going to have a son this time."

So we went back after that second winter. Kenny started guiding again and I waited for the birth of my son. We were in the big cabin then. We must have moved in that fall, and we still didn't have two boats or anything.

Bob was born in May. One morning I got up and I said to Kenny (he was going guiding) "You know, I don't feel too good this morning. I think the baby is coming today."

He said, "I have to go guiding anyway. If things get worse you will just have to take the boat and go down and I will watch for you."

Luckily, Mike Deschampe had brought me over this old boat about the week before. I told him when he was over to the house I didn't have a boat. I was a little bit scared there with Kenny gone all day and I had Barbara. So he brought me an old motor and an old boat that leaked pretty bad.

Anyway, that morning I knew Bob was coming that day so I got up and washed all Kenny's clothes, baked bread, and got everything ready so he would have something to eat. We had this old washing machine that had a motor on it, and I had to carry water from the lake and heat it first in a boiler on the stove and then put it in the washing machine and get an old washtub for rinsing. I got that all done. So about eleven o'clock or close to noon I knew I had to get going so I loaded that little crib in the boat and got my bailing can and took off.

It was lucky the motor started. Anyway, I got down by Saganaga Falls, and I saw a boat over there and I just knew it was Kenny fishing. He could see me but the funniest part of it was he told those tourists his wife must be going to have the baby today because she is going out.

These tourists said, "Let's get going. Let's get going. Get down there and get her to the hospital."

They said later, Kenny never got excited about anything. He just said, "That's okay. It's going to take her about an hour to get down there, forty-five minutes anyway, with that boat and motor. We'll have time to fill out your licenses." Those people were so nervous.

I got down to the landing and my sister was working at Chick Wauk Lodge then. Art Nunstedt still owned that place. I went up and told Janette, "I've really got labor pains and they are getting closer all the time."

That really scared her. She had a little room up above the store, and she told me to go up there and lay down until Kenny gets here. We didn't have a car. He had to borrow something or other to get me to town. We were going to go to Thunder Bay. I can't understand why but that was where we were going to go; hoping the kids would be Canadian so they could trap, I guess. I really don't know why we went clear to Thunder Bay.

So I went upstairs and laid down in this little room. Things weren't the best. I remember Janette would come and check on me every so often. Lydia Nunstedt was in a tizzy because Kenny wasn't there yet, and maybe Art would have to run me into town. They didn't have a hospital in Grand Marais then or anything. It would have to have been Two Harbors then. But finally here came Kenny. So I went down to meet him.

My pains were getting close then and I said, "We just got to get going, Kenny. I don't know if we can make it to town."

He said, "Geeze I got to clean the fish and get the shore dinner dishes all cleaned up and everything."

He had three guys with him, and they said, "You get the hell out of here. Get your wife to town. We can do all that. We will wash the dishes, clean the fish, ice them down, and clean the boats." They just wanted me to get out of there.

So, anyhow, we didn't have a car so he had to find a car. Too bad he didn't tell them or they would have taken us or given us their car just to get me going. Anyway, Kenny went up and talked to Art. He loaned us his '49 Ford station wagon with bald tires. We took off with this thing and we got about half way down to Grand Marais, and I said to Kenny. "Man, I don't know if I am going to make it."

Of course, he was getting a little nervous then. It just reminded me of these cops and robbers. We were just going around corners on two wheels. I was thinking, "I don't know if I am going to make this or not."

He stopped at Poplar Lake and he called the county nurse. Her name was Sarah Allard. She was going to meet us in Grand Marais and then go on to Thunder Bay with us in case something happened.

When we got to Grand Marais we had to run up to Ken's mothers house to leave Barbara off, and that took some time. Anyway, we got on our way and Sarah went with us. I felt a lot safer then, because I knew if the baby came at least I would have someone with me that knew what they were doing. I wasn't too sure about Kenny.

We got down to Thunder Bay, and it was really good we had the nurse with us because she went in to the hospital and they got me in right away.

I no more than got in the hospital and Bob was born. I was really glad we got there. He was skinny and scrawny when he was born. He was born about three weeks premature and he was just covered with hair. Oh, man, when the doctor put him on my stomach and said, "You have a beautiful son," I just started to cry. "Oh, my God," I thought.

"He looks like a monkey all covered with hair," I said.

The doctor said, "Oh, no, don't worry about that. It's premature and in a few days it will be all gone."

That was true for in a couple of days he was just a beautiful boy. I was really happy; I had my little boy then. Kenny went back home and went back to his guiding and I was only in the hospital four days. I got out of the hospital and was only at Muriel's a couple of days, I flew home that time too. I was so happy to get home. Then Kenny went down to Grand Marais to get Barbara, and then we had our whole family together.

I didn't know what I was getting into then with two little ones. Barbara was just eleven months old when Bob was born. I had my hands full that summer. I don't think I had much time to get lonesome or bored or anything else. Washing diapers and feeding kids took up my time. I was better at it then for I already had one baby, but I still had a lot to learn. I broke out with hives all over my body and I didn't know what it was because I had never seen hives before.

Kenny was gone, and I broke out with all this rash all over me. I swelled up and looked awful. There was no way I could get any place and I didn't dare touch the kids or anything because I thought I must have some terrible disease. Finally, my mom came down to see me, and I was crying there and she said, "What's the matter with you?"

I said, "Look, I've got some terrible disease. I'm covered with rash. I itch so terrible bad."

She ran up to Jock Richardson's. There happened to be a doctor up at Jock's so she brought the doctor back down with her. He took one look at me. "There is nothing serious wrong with you," he said. "You have got the hives. Have you been eating any strawberries?"

I said, "No."

"Well," he said. "It is either from an allergy or from nerves. Is anything bothering you?"

I told him, "Not really, but I have two little ones here and no boat or motor and my husband is gone from early morning to late at night."

He looked at me and said, "Hey, you have lots to be concerned about. I just can't imagine you even staying here with these two little kids in case anything should happen."

Anyhow, Mom took him back to the landing. He called Grand Marais and got a prescription up for me, and within two days I was all cleared up. I was really happy about that because I was really scared when that happened. That summer was a busy summer.

Barbara, Bill and Bob - mid 1950's

THREE IS ENOUGH

We were spending our third winter in Grand Marais. I was getting pretty good at having babies and on January 19, 1954, my second son, Bill was born.

I woke up on a stormy morning. I told Kenny he better not go to work that day, as I knew the baby was going to be born. Two Harbors, some eighty-five miles away was the nearest hospital. Fortunately, my sister Janette was staying with us, so we had our baby-sitter.

I asked Janette, "Do you think you can handle two kids?"

She said, "Don't you worry about a thing. There's nothing to it."

Kenny called his folks to tell them we were going to the hospital. His dad, Victor, wanted to go with us. He'd lost his first wife when she gave birth to their third child, and this being my third, he was very worried about me.

By the time the three of us arrived, I was well into my labor. Dr. Moyer took blood tests and said I would need two pints of blood because I was very anemic. This really worried Kenny's Dad. Lots of frightening memories must have been going through his mind.

I have a rather rare blood type, so it was difficult to find two donors. There were no blood banks then, so if you needed blood, someone had to be called in to donate. The doctor said he would have to prolong my labor until they found two donors. "Just stay calm and don't do any pushing or anything," he told me. Easy for him to say!

It seemed like forever to find the donors and wait for the transfusions, but finally, they said I could have the baby. In a short time, the baby was born and Dr. Moyer said, "You have a beautiful son."

Kenny's dad was so relieved, and he asked if we would name our baby after his second son, William, who was a doctor. He thought that would be a good omen. So we named our boy William Victor.

After about five days in the hospital, Kenny came down to pick our new son and me up. On the way home, we pretty well decided, God willing, that this would be our last baby.

When we arrived home from the hospital, Janette's first words were, "Thank goodness you're home!" I asked her what was wrong and she said, "I don't know how you do it. Bob tipped over a plant and ate some of the leaves before I could get to him, then he helped the dog eat part of the dog food and I just don't know how you're going to make it now with three of them."

Janette headed for home after a few more days, having had enough of baby-sitting. Bill turned out to be a very good baby, so we made out just fine.

THE MODEL-T

Kenny had this old Model-T Ford coupe that he bought when he was about fourteen years old. It was still on his parent's farm when we got married, but he insisted on bringing it up to our cabin so we could use it in the wintertime after the lake had froze over. It took two of us to start that thing in the winter when it was cold.

We went down to the farm the following summer and drove that thing back up the trail. It got a flat tire somewhere around Gunflint Lake. It didn't have a spare, so we drove it on a flat tire about twelve more miles to Saganaga. Art Nunstedt let us store it at Chick Wauk Lodge until the following winter. In the meantime, Kenny bought two new "knobby" tires to put on the rear so he could drive it eight miles across the lake to our cabin the following winter.

After the lake had frozen over to be safe for travel, we took our dog team down to Chick Wauk to get The Car. I learned to hate that thing that day, because it took us about two hours just to get it started! He had drained the block and the radiator when he parked it there in the summer, because we couldn't afford real antifreeze. Alcohol was a lot cheaper, but it had a low boiling point. So that wouldn't work either.

First of all, we had to chop a hole through the ice to get water for the radiator. After we had a couple of pails of water, Kenny actually lifted one rear wheel, while I put a block under the axle! He said, "That will make it easier to crank!" Then he built a small fire under the engine to warm up the oil. It's a wonder that the whole thing didn't burn up.

While the oil was warming up, he gave me instructions as to what I had to do once he started cranking. It had a starter, but the battery was dead. You should have seen all the levers and pedals in that thing! It didn't have an automatic transmission or even a clutch! It didn't even have a gas pedal! Of course, I didn't know how to drive anyway, so at the time I thought this must be the way it's supposed to be.

I remember, first, he had to turn the choke. He said, "That's to enrich the mixture for starting." Then he went on to explain the spark and throttle levers, which were just under the steering wheel, one on each side. He set them in their proper position. He explained all I had to do when he was cranking and when (and if) it fired, I was to pump the choke and pump those two levers until it started running on its own.

It seemed awfully complicated to me, but he reassured me there was nothing to it. Oh, how he lied! There was this lever sticking up through the floor on the left side. He said, "That's the neutral lever. If you pull it all the way back, it's also the parking brake. Just make sure it's only back part way when I start cranking." Then there was the key. He said, "Normally you put it on battery to start, then once it starts, you switch it over to mag, but we won't do that today because the battery is dead anyway."

Well, after all those instructions, the motor felt a little warm. He filled the radiator. He said, "I sure hope it starts before the water freezes in the radiator." After he filled the radiator, he put out the fire under the engine. I took up my position as driver and he went over the operating procedure once more. Once he began to crank, every time his head came up over the radiator, he would bark a new command! After a considerable amount of cranking and a few backfires, which he said was because I advanced the spark too far, the old thing started. Though the sweat was running down his face, I can still see his proud smile.

As it was early in the winter, there wasn't too much snow on the ground or on the ice. So Kenny drove his old Model-T and I drove our dog team. As I recall, I didn't have any trouble keeping up, because he had to go in low gear all the way. Once we got home, he had to drain the water out again.

A month or so went by when one nice day, Kenny suggested we crank up the 'T and go visit my mom. It was about three miles to her place and it had snowed a lot since we had brought that thing up across the ice. I suggested we take the dog team, but he wouldn't hear of it. He reassured me that with those old knobbies on her, she would go anyplace.

I dreaded to think of going through all the motions to start that old car again. Our little daughter, Barb, was only about eight months old at the time, so the thought of riding in a car instead of going by dog team had some merit.

This time he not only heated the oil in the engine, but heated the water for the radiator as well. After the water was put in and the oil was warm (he even built a little fire under the rear end this time), he went over the starting procedure once again. I was not very enthusiastic about all this, because it would have been so much simpler to just take the dog team to my mother's, but he was very determined — maybe stubborn would be a better word!

Once he started cranking, it was just like before; a new command every time his head came up above the radiator. When it started to fire, I thought he said I was supposed to jerk on the spark lever. Well, I jerked on it all right. It backfired and the crank slipped out of his hand and hit him alongside the head! He went down like a ton of bricks. But it wasn't long before he was up and sporting a big lump on his head. He was more determined than ever. Finally we got it going, so he was grinning from ear to ear.

We bundled up the baby, got in the old 'T and started across the lake. The snow wasn't too deep for the first mile or so, but when we got out where the snow had drifted it was another story! We got stuck so many times, as Kenny would try to back up and hit her again. Finally that old 'T threw a rod or something, so we had to walk home about a mile and a half without snowshoes. Boy, was I mad! Kenny's biggest concern was how he was going to get his old car back home. That was the first and last trip I took in that old car.

The next morning Kenny thought maybe, under the circumstances, Jock Richardson, whose island resort was about three miles away just might let him borrow his horse. He knew this wouldn't be easy, trying to talk Jock out of his horse, because he had tried to rent it from him before to skid our saw logs out to the lake. Jock always bragged about that horse, how smart he was, all he had to do to drive him was to holler Gee or Haw, Giddyup or Whoa.

Kenny grew up on a farm and had been driving horses since he was five or six years old, so he knew something about horses. It took a lot of convincing to assure Jock that he was very qualified to handle a horse. Finally Jock reluctantly agreed to let him take the horse, but laid down some pretty strict conditions. One of which was that he didn't want his horse coming back all lathered up from sweat. He also didn't want Kenny to ride him because the horse didn't like anyone on his back. So Kenny started out on snowshoes, first driving the horse, but the horse didn't really want to go in that direction. Kenny ended up snowshoeing ahead of the horse while he lead him with a rope. It was here where he began to doubt this horse's intelligence.

When he got to the Model-T, he put his snowshoes in the trunk, knowing from here on he could just steer his car while the horse pulled him home. He said he opened the windshield so he could talk to the horse. He hooked the horse up to the car, hung the lines around the hames (collar), then got into the car and hollered, "Giddyup" to the horse, quickly followed by, "Haw, haw, haw. Haw, damn it! Haw!"

Well, it seems being that the car was already pointed in the direction of Jock's and that was where the horse wanted to go anyway, that was the direction they took for quite a ways before Kenny could get out and actually run the horse down, get the lines, and get him turned around. From then on, he ran the lines in under the windshield so he could steer the horse. Eventually they got home with the old Model-T.

It was quite late in the afternoon when he got back to our cabin and he still had to take the horse back to Jock's. He was so tired by that time, he just couldn't imagine snowshoeing clear over to Jock's and back, so he came up with another one of his good ideas. He decided to hook the horse up to the toboggan we normally used for the dog teams.

This toboggan was a homemade affair, made much like a ski, about eight feet long, fifteen inches wide, with a rope attached near the front. This was what most of the dog team drivers used at the time because it was light and fast. You just stood on it and held onto the rope.

He put the harness on three dogs, tied one front leg up on each dog so they couldn't run, then tied them to the back end of the toboggan. I had to help hold the dogs while he got everything ready to go.

He knew he wouldn't have to steer the horse as long as he was headed home, so he again wrapped the lines around the hames. I guess he thought the horse was more tired than he was, so he assumed the horse would just walk along, pulling the toboggan, and the dogs would just limp along behind while he stood on the toboggan enjoying the ride. Then he could hitch the dogs to the toboggan after he had returned the horse and have a good ride home.

If you've ever been around sled dogs when you hitch them up, you know when you give the signal, it's as if they are shot out of a cannon! Well, even though each dog had one front leg tied up when Kenny said, "Okay, giddyup," and I let those dogs loose it didn't matter! They took off barking and jerked the toboggan right from under Kenny. I don't know if the dogs were trying to catch the horse or what, but he wasn't waiting around to find out! Kenny still had a hold of the rope on the toboggan and was taking about eight foot strides, hollering, "Whoa, whoa, whoa, whoa," but the horse wasn't listening! It was by far, the fastest Kenny had ever run!

After about a quarter of a mile he had to let go of the rope. All he could do was watch as those poor dogs tumbled behind the toboggan. About a quarter of a mile further the dogs broke loose and the horse kept going.

After retrieving the dogs, Kenny came home, hooked them up to another sled and headed for Jock's. He dreaded going over there to face Jock, knowing how he worshipped his horse. It was well after dark when he got over to Jock's. He found what was left of the toboggan up near the barn. Jock was still in the barn, wiping the sweat off his horse.

When he told Jock what had happened, he thought he might get some sympathy, but there was none. Jock told him that his horse would probably catch pneumonia and die. The horse recovered. Kenny felt bad about it and didn't think that was a good time to question the horse's ability to understand what "Whoa" meant. After that episode, my mom used to listen for that old Model-T on nice winter days, worrying that we might try it again.

Kenny with his Model-T at their home on Saganaga

A FUN SUMMER —
GRANDMA, GRANDPA AND GUIDING

It was the spring of 1953. We had just moved back to our cabin at Red Sucker Bay on Saganaga. We had spent the winter in Grand Marais, where Kenny drove a pulp truck for his uncle. Although we had built our home on Saganaga, and had plans to eventually build a small resort there, it was tough trying to make a living with only sporadic guiding jobs. We spent the winter of '50-51 and '51-52 at our place on Saganaga. After that we moved to Grand Marais each fall for the next couple of winters. Each spring we couldn't wait to return to our cabin on Saganaga to pursue our dreams.

By the spring of '53 we already had two children, with a third on the way. It was lonely for me at our cabin, with Kenny guiding almost every day. When Mom asked us if Grandma and Grandpa could stay in our first little cabin while she and Irv were building a cabin for them on the east end of "Jock's" island, I said, "Gee, Mom, that would be just great!"

Until this spring Grandma and Grandpa had lived in the family home on Saganagons. During the past two summers, since my Mom had married and moved to Saganaga, it was really tough for her to take care of them. Nearly every evening, after coming home from guiding all day, she would go over to the portage by Uncle Frank's, carry whatever supplies they needed over that two-and-one-half-mile portage, then paddle an old canvas canoe from the portage about a half mile over to where Grandpa and Grandma lived. After looking in on them she would head back to Saganaga well after dark. That was how devoted my mom was to her parents.

So when Irv and Mom decided to build Grandma and Grandpa a cabin on Saganaga, Kenny and I were happy to have them stay in our little cabin for the summer. It would be good for everyone. My Mom wouldn't have to make all those trips across that long portage to Saganagons and I would have company all summer. Grandpa could paddle his canoe the two miles to where Irv and Mom were building the new cabin. It was the nicest summer I ever had there. Once in awhile I got a guiding job. Grandma was there to watch the kids for me. It must have been quite a handful for her because Barb and Bob were only two and one years old, She was happy to do it, though, so I could go make some "big money."

So I started guiding once in a while. That was a comedy in itself. I'd go down to the landing and I would follow Kenny around. I didn't know Saganaga. If we had been on Saganagons, I knew where all the rocks were and the shallow places.

Kenny would usually have the men of a party and I would have the women. I would take off with him and the worst place I ever went was up the rapids on Seagull River. He would go up those rapids lickety-split and I would try to follow him but I would be hitting the rocks. I just hated it so I would go up there just a couple of times.

I made out real good with the guiding. We went out to Blueberry Hole, fishing trout, one time. Freddy Drouillard was out there and so was Kenny. They were big-time guides and here I am, coming along, not really knowing what I am doing. I knew how to fish and all that but not *where* to fish. When I was a kid, we just put down a hook almost any place and we would catch fish. It was not this way anymore.

We went out in Blueberry Hole. It was a beautiful day, and I had the two nicest ladies. Kenny kept pointing over here and over there, and Freddy was laughing. I was fishing someplace over there but I wasn't in the right hole. Wouldn't you know, my party caught some nice trout and then on my way back into the landing we stopped in the narrows.

I told my ladies, "Let's stop here and see if we can get some walleyes." We filled out on walleyes like you can't believe.

We were very lucky. Kenny didn't have his limit. These women were kidding their husbands because when the men saw me they wondered what this little kid was going to do. I really *wasn't* very old, but I probably looked even younger.

Those ladies were so nice I told them about my life and my kids and everything. They said, "When we get home we are going to send you a whole box of clothes for your babies." When they went home they sent me a box of clothes. You can't believe it. They were just beautiful. I had all kinds of things for the kids. We had sweaters and just everything.

One time I left Kenny and he was going to do the wash. Mike Deschampe always seemed to be mixed up with what we did. He was so good to us and we treasured that, especially me. He would just do anything for me. Anyhow, he came down and I was gone someplace. Kenny said, "I got to wash clothes, Mike. What shall I do with all this?" Mike said, "Just throw it all in the boiler and boil it." When I got back there were the beautiful sweaters, diapers, and everything all different colors. There were reds and pinks on the night shirts. He boiled it on the stove and hung it out. That was the last time I ever let him do the wash.

That summer was a very precious summer. Grandma and Grandpa made out just fine. They lived in that little cabin near us until their cabin was finished.

Grandma with Bob and Barbara

JANETTE AND I TAKE A TRIP

Janette went down to the county landing and some fellow had seen her down there and took pictures of her and her dog team. She was such a beautiful girl when she was young. She still is beautiful.

They wrote her and told her they wanted her to come down to Toronto and kick off the Easter Seal Drive. Well, she called me. I was in Grand Marais, and she said, "Betty, you got to go with me. I'm not going to go alone."

I talked to Kenny. We'd had Bill by that time but Kenny figured he could handle things while I was gone. So I said, "Okay, this will be an experience and we will have fun."

Anyhow, they contacted Wieben, a Canadian pilot from Superior Airways. He was to pick us up on Saganaga in front of my mom's house. Wieben was a very nice man and he did so much for us when we were kids —he would bring us things.

He landed in there, and we took three dogs and our sleds. Wieben was so mad at my mom. He thought this was the worst thing she ever let her daughters do, to go to Toronto with the three dogs.

He picked us up at Saganaga and we flew into Thunder Bay with these dogs that have never been out anyplace. They had always been up there in the woods. We had arranged to get kennels for them and everything. Wieben helped us and that night he took us out to dinner. He begged us not to go. He said that he just didn't

want to see us going to Toronto. He gave us his address and tele-
phone number and he said, "If you get into any trouble call me and
I'll come right down there and get you." Anyhow he put us on the
train to go from Thunder Bay to Toronto.

We had never been on a train before. We started out. We
had our dogs back in the boxcars. Of course, they were petrified
with all this and we weren't much better. We got on this train and
we had the upper berth and lower berth. First, we went back and fed
our dogs. We spent a lot of time with those dogs and sat back there
with them. We just liked being with them. We'd be talking about
everything and what was coming, scared in a way but excited about
what was going to happen.

Anyhow, we crawled into bed that night. Janette was on
the lower birth, and I was on the upper berth. The porters and the
people were walking through, and all we had was a curtain. Janette
got scared because she could see men's legs walking by. She crawled
up in that upper berth and we both slept there all night. There wasn't
enough room for *one* person.

We got into Toronto about eight o'clock the next night.
The men were there to meet us. They took pictures of Janette with
roses and all this stuff, and they told me to get in the sled, and
Janette could drive the dogs out of the train depot. We told them
there is no way these dogs are going to start going on this bare pave-
ment. They had lines of people. They must have advertised this
about these girls coming from the backwoods with their dog team
down here in Toronto. We tried to talk them out of it, but no way.

All these people were lined up. I said to this one guy,
"Let me hold the dogs."

"No, no," he said, "You just get in the sled and go."

One old guy was eating a sandwich there. So our dog,
O'Cheek, just went up and took that sandwich out of that guy's
hand. It scared that guy half to death.

Well, we made it out of there and they took us to this
great big hotel, checked us in, and they wouldn't let us go anyplace.
They had a public relations man there who took us everywhere and
looked after us. We were just with this public relations fellow. I
didn't know what was going on and neither did Janette. Wieben had
told us not to drink anything unless it was a can of pop. If it wasn't

in a can, they might put a pill in it or something. We didn't dare drink anything unless we drank water in our room. We couldn't go to a restaurant by ourselves. They were there to pick us up in the morning and take us back to the hotel in the evening.

The next day we got our dogs over to the kennel. They took us down to this big department store, and we each got a parka and a nice long dress — we got all kinds of clothes. We must have had a couple hundred dollars worth of clothes, each. Gee, we thought we were queens of the world then.

They told us we were going to go down and cook a pancake breakfast so we had to get all these fancy duds on. We went down there and we cooked this breakfast. People were flocking around us and asking questions of us. You know, we really didn't know what was going on. We just knew that we were getting treated pretty good.

Anyway, we got done with that and we went back to the hotel. It was really a nice place, but I can't recall the name of the hotel. It was right downtown Toronto, I know that. Every night they would take us out to dinner, then we would get ready to go to bed at night and words of Wieben would come back, "Be awful careful down there, you girls, because you don't know what this is all about. It might be just a big scam."

Janette would pile all the furniture in front of the door. I think she sat up most of the night. She was scared to death. I was never that scared so I slept. I'd wake up at night and there she would be sitting in a chair with all the furniture piled around her against the door.

When we went out to dinner we would always have to dress up and go out to these nice restaurants. Then we would hear Wieben's words, "Don't drink anything unless it is in a can or water in your motel room." They would offer to get us a cocktail. Well, we didn't drink anyway so we'd say no and they would say, "Well, what kind of pop would you like." We answered "canned pop" But we were told they didn't have canned pop here. Well, then we just wanted water. "Oh, no," we would think. "We can't drink water either for they might put a pill in that."

The next day we were supposed to go in this parade. So we got our dogs all hitched up. We kept telling these people that these dogs are not going to do what we want them to do. They would say that we could handle it and to just do what they told us to do. I said, "Why don't you just go ahead and let me hold the dogs?" No, no, they didn't want that.

So here we start out with these dogs. They were just panicky. We started and, wouldn't you know, on the next street down here comes this old horse with a milk wagon. I said to Janette, "Oh, I'm scared. I don't know what is going to happen when we get to where the horse is."

Janette had her brake on trying to hold the dogs, but they spotted that old horse and, holy smokes, the dogs took off. Janette had the brake on and I couldn't get out because we were going too fast. Boy, we were traveling. We went by all these old people with their parade. The dogs took after this old horse. That old man that had the milk wagon had milk scattered all over, for when the horse took off there was no stopping it either.

Finally some Mounties stopped the dogs. We told them we just had to hold those dogs. We just couldn't drive them down the main street because they weren't used to seeing all this stuff. They were just from the bush back there.

Then the Mounties stayed pretty close to us and they took good care of us after that. They understood that we had come from the woods and didn't understand everything going on around us. They tried to help us the best way they could.

They had all of this in the papers, but they wouldn't let us see the papers. They just let us see what they wanted us to see. So I don't believe it was what they said it was supposed to be. It was a big parade and I don't know if it was an Easter parade or what.

When we got back to our hotel that night we were just exhausted fighting with all the elements out there — with the dogs being scared, and just everything. We got back to our room and they were going to take us out to dinner but we said, "No we didn't want dinner, we were too tired. We're going to bed."

We no more than got into bed and they called us from the kennels. They said one of our dogs was very ill. They wanted to know, could we come over there because he was having convulsions and was very sick? The dog wasn't the only one that was sick — we were sick too.

We went downstairs. There was one thing we weren't supposed to do and that was to go without this public relations man. We never even called him.

The fellow that was driving the taxi said, "Gee, aren't you the girls who are from the bush?" We said we were. He said, "Isn't it awful cold when you chop a hole in the lake and just go for a swim."

I said. "We don't chop a hole."

"Oh," he said, "There are some articles in the paper with pictures before and after going swimming."

Then we started to realize what they had put in those newspapers. I don't know why we just didn't tell him to go out and get us some newspapers but at that time we were more concerned about our dog.

When we got over there O'Cheek was really sick but when he saw us he just started to get better. We sat over there with the dog until three o'clock in the morning. Before we got there the dog was so excited that the people at the kennel couldn't give him the necessary tranquilizers because they were afraid that he would bite them. When he saw us he started to calm right down and they were able to give him the medicine. We stayed until three and then took a cab back to the hotel. We talked about all of this, and we wondered what was really going on.

The following day we played our guitars and sang in a store window. That was a fun day, and we met a lot of people. We had fun, and then that night we were going to take the train and head home. We were there four days and three nights.

That night we got our stuff all packed up. They had given us each so much money to spend, I think it was like $200 a piece and we spent most of it.

The public relations man drove us to the train that night. He gave us the story how he didn't make any money and we should give him back what money we had left. As he was going on, Janette felt sorry for him so she gave him all her money. I told Janette we had to have some money to get back home. All we had was what I had left (which wasn't much), but our train tickets were paid for.

We enjoyed our trip home a lot more. We weren't so scared and we knew Wieben was going to meet us at the train and fly us back to Saganaga. We would go back and sit with our dogs on the train. We met some hobos. We never met any hobos before but we sort of fit in with them because we were kind of hobos too.

We got to talking to this one man. He was the nicest person. He rode the box cars but he told us not to tell anybody they were back there. He'd feed the dogs for us. He gave us a little can opener. We didn't have a can opener. I still have that can opener. They were both the nicest guys. We spent most of our time back there visiting with them instead of up on the front part of the train.

Wieben picked us up at the train depot. He was so glad, and when he saw us, he was just smiling and so happy that we had made it back. We flew back into Saganaga that same day we arrived. That was really an experience.

Tempest, Dick Powell, Orville Weiben, Betty, Janette and Minerva with dogs, O'Cheek, King and Buster

MY FINAL TRANSITION
TO THE OUTSIDE WORLD

In 1954 we made our big move out of Saganaga. We left our place up there and moved to Hovland. We purchased an old farm. It wasn't a very hard move for me because it was on 80 acres of land and was really very remote. We didn't have any running water and had to use an outside biffy. There was a well that we got all of our water from. It was easy for me to adjust to this after living in the woods. We lived there for three or four years. We didn't even have electricity when we moved in there. Eventually we got electricity.

From there we moved to Tofte, where Kenny got a job with Erie Mining Company. We bought our first modern home and that was kind of a funny thing. We got this home and moved in. This was so unreal to me because I wasn't used to having running water or flush toilets, you know. It was just so *easy*.

Kenny came home one day from work and I was crying. He said, "What's the matter with you?"

I said, "There is nothing to do here. I don't even have to carry water, or heat water for the wash, or carry wood in to build a fire."

Everything was just at my finger tips. It was real hard for me to get used to that type of life at first, but eventually I did for I had three little ones to take care of and so, I was busy anyway.

We lived in that house for quite a few years and I worked at Edgewater Motel for fifteen years as a waitress while my children were growing up. When I was about 37 years old, Bill, my last child, left home. That was a very hard change for me — to learn how to occupy my time. I had been so used to being busy.

So, a little resort came up for sale at Ilgen City. As we would drive by we would see this sign for sale that said "Population Four, Room for More." We kept thinking we should check on that so we went down there and checked in and decided to buy this place.

We started to purchase it in the fall and by spring we moved to Ilgen City. At one time Ilgen City was owned and operated by Rudy Ilgen and his wife. It consisted of a large building decorated with a southwest Indian decor. It was a halfway stop between Grand Marais and Duluth where meals were served. It also was located on a corner where a road went north to Finland. The building burned down and was never replaced. Eventually a motel was constructed in the vicinity of that old building site.

The building wasn't in very good shape when we bought it so we literally had to overhaul the whole place. We loved it there. We had twenty five acres to ourselves and we had three cabins, eight motel units, a basement apartment and a beautiful home. It was the nicest home I had ever lived in. It had all cedar paneling on the inside, a beautiful view of the lake, and you could always see the sunrise come up. Really, I was quite happy in this place until all the motel guests started arriving. With no formal education I had to learn to run a resort and deal with people.

I never realized what it was like to be with people. I could go to bed at night and if I had a no vacancy sign out, at two or three in the morning someone would rap on the door and want a room. I would tell them, "I'm sorry but we are all full."

They would say, "How much are your rooms?"

I would say, "We don't have any rooms, they are all full."

They would repeat, "How much are your rooms?"

Finally, I would tell them our rates and they would say they couldn't pay that much for a room. I would think, "I had just told them we didn't have a room so why would they worry paying for it."

We had quite some experiences in that motel and I don't think I would have ever made it without the help of Stanley Johnson. We employed Stanley a couple of years after we got the place. He was an old fellow and he became part of that place with me. He was always there to help me with almost anything.

The minute the guests would go out, he would be in their room, stripping the beds. A few times, he even stripped beds before they checked out; they were just going for breakfast. We had many laughs together over things like that.

I cried with him a lot, too. Kenny was working at Erie then. It seemed like he was always gone when something went wrong. One time, when we had a bad leak in the basement, Kenny was on the afternoon shift so I ran over and got Stan to help. Stanley put his thumb over the leak and I just stood there crying. He just looked at me and said, "Quit your damn crying and do something. I'm drowning here."

One time, Stanley thought the pressure had gotten to me and I'd surely lost my mind. We were trying to trap what we thought was a martin or some other small animal, that had been getting into our garbage. Three days in a row, the trap was sprung, but nothing was trapped.

My mom said it was probably a bear so we'd better just take our trap and forget it. That had to be the most disastrous day of my life. The fish bag we'd been using for bait had been hanging for those three days. When I reached up to get it, it broke and the rotten fish fell all over my head. I have such a weak stomach.

Stan hadn't seen what happened. I just took off and started running for home. On my way, I started peeling off my clothes. Stan was standing on the hill and saw me. When he got to the house and found out what happened, he said, "Oh, Betty! I was sure I would have to call the police. I thought you'd flipped your lid for sure."

One time we had some fishermen from Canada. They used to stop on their way up and on their way back and stay overnight. They came in and I asked them how their fishing was. They said, "Oh, great." They got all their limits and they asked me if I thought it was all right to leave the fish in the boats.

We had never had any problems and I said, "I don't think there is any problem." That night here comes this bear, and he tore up their coolers and fish. It just totally wiped them all out of their fishing trip. I felt so bad about that. So every once in a while we would have that kind of trouble.

Another time we had my little niece that stayed with us for about three summers. She helped us with the motel. We had a little buck deer at that time we called Bambi. He moved in with us. They had it on TV, and everything.

This little deer just took a liking to my niece. She could just call him and he would come and be with her and play hide and seek with her. It was so neat for the tourists because they would be in their rooms and Bambi would come right up on the porch. He would walk and look in the windows begging for stuff, wanting them to give him doughnuts or whatever they had.

That deer stayed with us for most of the summer. It was so much fun having that deer with us. The only trouble was he ate every kind of flower I had and ate everything out of our garden. He would jump right over anything we put around the garden. He even ate the rose bushes. I never knew they ate rose bushes too

Later on that summer he crossed the highway and got hit and broke both hind legs. We rushed him down to the vet but they had to put him to sleep. That really crushed our little niece. It is hard to have a wild animal that is tame near the highway because the cars just go too fast. We saw so many deer killed at our place there.

We fed all the deer on the upper side of the road. We had up to 60 deer sometimes in our backyard. We got so we called them by name. It was always so strange — when the hunting season started, those deer left. Many of them would come back after deer season, but not the young ones. The older ones that knew about hunting season came back. I think we had one old doe we called Betsy and for four years it came back every fall.

It was nice to see the animals, just like cattle coming to be fed. We could never have any bushes of any kind, they would eat everything up. I had a sewing room that faced the backyard and the deer would lie all over the side of the hill. I just couldn't shoot a deer the whole time we were in that business. If I fed them, I surely couldn't go out and shoot them. That ended my deer hunting.

We had many happy days in our little resort but there were many frustrating days too. I guess the only reason I even fit in that situation was that I was in the woods and I'm always at home in the woods. It seems like anything that I do, if I am near the forest I am okay.

I guess I knew when I had to get out of that business because I was getting real frustrated with people. I love people but when I never have time to myself . . . I guess that is what made us decide to sell.

Kenny retired in 1987 on Thanksgiving Day. Our children were all home and that was a happy day. I wasn't too sure how things were going to go. We decided to sell the motel and buy a mobile home to retire in and then go south every winter. In 1988 we moved to our little home up on a hill. It overlooks the Baptism River and it is just gorgeous. Around us, it is all forest. We live in an area where there are no homes except behind us. We watch the deer and bear and wolves across the river.

It is just so unique, and we love it. When we first sold our home and moved up on the hill here, I just cried for days. I didn't know how I was going to go from this big home with three bedrooms, big living room and fireplace, into a mobile home. We had to get rid of most of our things and I just thought that was the worst. All of my friends told me I wasn't going to be happy up there nor happy in that mobile home. Well, I tell you, we moved in here and I wouldn't go back to a home for anything. This is just so easy to keep clean. We have more time to do things we want to do. We can close it up in the winter and go south, which we do because we have a trailer down there too.

THE FINALÉ

My life is quite unique now in my older age. I know it is coming to a close and yet I am just so happy here. I have what I've always dreamed of. A little home on top of a hill overlooking a valley or river or lake or something.

I hope this book will help other people. If you come from a background like I did, you can still go out and fit in the *outside* world. It is the culture problem that is hard to cope with, but I try to tell Kenny all the time, it's not coming from that backwoods so much; it's trying to blend the two cultures.

I grew up with an Indian grandma. We lived her Indian ways a lot. It was hard to fit into the white man's way and still is. I have my beliefs, what I like to do and, sometimes, it doesn't really fit in the white people's culture. I am married to a Norwegian-Swede and their heritage is so different. We have had our ups and downs trying to work out the differences of our two, diverse backgrounds. Some were quick to judge, saying our marriage would never last. Well, there have been some bumps along the way, but we are celebrating our forty-sixth year together this fall.

I often think of my grandma and grandpa. I believe pressure had gotten to them and that is why they moved back up in the woods. He was English and Irish and she was Ojibwa and couldn't even speak English, but that didn't stop them from getting married and raising five children.

I'm very proud of my family. They did real well for not having college educations. Even my uncles did quite well building resorts and cabins. They made a good living for their families. It is totally different now than when I was a kid and lived on Saganagons. Every evening there would be beaver swimming by. There would be muskrats and otter or ducks, and loons, too. We could go over to the little river that runs into Saganagons and paddle up that river and see beaver eating in the river or moose diving. It was just great back then.

Now I don't hear partridge drumming like I used to. The one bird that I miss so much, that I used to hear as a child, is a night hawk. He used to be out there buzzing around the house at night hunting bugs. I haven't heard one for years. I seldom hear owls anymore.

We live in a State Forest now. There is a lot of wilderness area around here. Still, when the river freezes up in the fall, the only tracks we see now are from an occasional wolf, and deer. We don't see any of the little animal tracks around here any more. There are hardly any rabbits (we would sure have a tough life if we had to live off a rabbit population now). I seldom see a fox track and I don't ever see a grouse.

Now the woods are almost silent when I walk through them. I can remember when there were so many birds singing all the time. You can drive for miles before you can see or hear anything. That frightens me. It seems we have a lot of predators and not many of the other animals.

There is nothing wrong with the predator — except that the biggest predator around is man. The partridge season goes for three months and we seldom see a partridge. People are hunting with dogs and four wheelers. The partridge, and the other animals that have hunting seasons on them, haven't got a chance.

I don't know what is going to happen to our land. I'm afraid there isn't going to be much left for my children, grandchildren and great grandchildren unless mankind turns itself around and starts thinking of nature.

What would this world be like if there weren't any wild animals, birds? Everything would just be silent. Not a very good place to live.

A long time ago my grandma said, "Human beings are going to destroy this earth. It's going to go up in a big ball of fire. When the animals are gone, humans will be gone too."